The Ultimate Journey

HARNESSING THE POWER
OF STORYTELLING
FOR YOUR BUSINESS

By Matthew Mendelsohn

ISBN: 6027950587
eISBN: 978-602-7950-58-0

1. Marketing. 2. Storytelling. 3. Business. 4. Writing.

Jacket Design: Anida Dyah
Editing: Roy Simson

For my wife Joe and our little guy Liam. You remained patient waiting for me to finish this story and yet you are the other part of the greatest story in which I've ever been involved.

TABLE OF CONTENTS

ONE

LIFE IN A NORTHERN TOWN
The Story Behind This Story

ALFREDO: I choose my friends for their looks, and my enemies for their brains. You're too smart to be my friend. Besides, as I always tell my kids, be careful to pick the right friends!
SALVATORE: But you don't have any kids!
ALFREDO: All right, all right! When I've got kids that's what I'm telling them!

- Cinema Paradiso (1988)[1]

---

1 Cinema Paradiso. Dir. Guiseppe Tornatore. Miramax Films, 1988.

I would like to begin with a short story. This is about how ice hockey, bookmobiles and icy winters all came together to create this book.

When I was a kid, I was fascinated by geography. Perhaps my two most prized possessions were a globe and a world almanac. I used to spin the globe around really fast and stop it with one finger to see which random country I had landed on. Then I would run over to my almanac that contained details of all 161 countries on earth[2] and learn about this new country, the language they spoke, the industries they had, their population and most importantly, at what sports they excelled. I particularly liked looking at the full-color pages showing off the flags of each of these countries and imagining why they would choose those colors and designs. I think Sri Lanka was one of my favorites on account of the fact that it had a lion as its emblem and lots of colors. Perhaps Brazil was second on account of the fact that you just didn't find many flags with those vibrant yellow, green and blue colors.

Every week, there was this great initiative run by our local public library system in Toronto called the Bookmobile. It was kind of a mobile mini-library housed in a truck that would go each day from strip mall to strip mall and park for two or three hours before moving to a different location based on its weekly schedule. I remember always looking forward to trudging through the heavy snow in my winter coat, boots and thick mittens just to see the treasure trove of geography books inside. One of my favorites was a series of illustrated books depicting life in different countries, including how the average family spent their day and, again, what sports they played. I was most interested in the European countries like Sweden, Finland and the USSR, if for no other reason than they all had really good national ice hockey teams and...well, I was a Canadian kid.[3] Since we experienced something like eight months of winter, hockey was a really, really big deal for us.[4]

One thing that I got from reading all of those books was a certain sense of adventure aimed at experiencing other countries. Sadly, few of my classmates shared

---

2 If you can imagine, we once lived in a world that had only two 'stans (we didn't have Kazakhstan, Turkmenistan and all the others back then), two Germanys and where Yugoslavia was one country instead of about 20 (ok, I'm exaggerating). I just officially dated myself.

3 The Canadian national hockey team beating the USSR in 1972 still stands as one of the greatest moments in Canada's history, along with the 2010 Olympics hockey gold medal win over the US. Many find it interesting that we Canadians can relate a lot of our recent history to hockey-related moments. I suppose that tells you something about us Canucks.

4 Give us a break! We don't understand cricket, badminton, Australian Rules or any of those other foreign sports. Even our version of football awards a single point for simply booting a ball as far as possible.

this ambition. It seemed as if each of them wanted to graduate high school with the highest grades, go to one of the local universities or an Ivy League college, get their degree, get a master's, marry someone from their community, become a doctor or a lawyer, have 2.5 children, become a grandparent and grow old. It felt incredibly dull to me. I mean, where were the pirates and buccaneers, the buried treasure! Where was the adventure?

So I exaggerate a bit, but nevertheless, I was always thinking that we have such a short time on this earth. Why would we want to live a life that is the same as everyone else's?

When my close friend, Sheldon, celebrated his Bar Mitzvah, his Rabbi gave him a compliment during a speech to the congregation that I would forever envy: "One thing you can always say about Sheldon is that he's unique." I always felt this was the greatest compliment a person could ever receive.[5]

Sadly, "unique" people weren't generally very popular in high school (or in university for that matter). Had I been born five years later, I would have hit the internet dating boom just as it reached full force and being unique would have been a tremendous asset. Very likely, I could have become a very popular travel blogger at the very least.

I developed an intense desire to "write" my own story, experiencing a life that was uniquely mine. Everything I did thereafter was in the spirit of exploration. Thanks to these experiences, I developed a knack for noticing things. I started travelling the world, to countries as far-flung as Ghana, Cote d'Ivoire, Belgium, Indonesia, Taiwan, Thailand and Singapore, and during this time discovered that being a stranger in a strange land gave me a unique insight into well … just about everything. I started writing a journal and during one eight-month backpacking odyssey through Southeast Asia filled more than 1,000 pages recounting every experience, every sight and every chance encounter with a stranger on the street. I stopped viewing the world as a bunch of things, people and places and started seeing everything as if it was four-dimensional, with a 500-word story around every corner. I became, in short, a sucker for a good (or for that matter, any) story. And while I was developing into a pretty skilled writer, it was my sense of curiosity that made me even sharper (in addition to almost getting me killed in a few cases).

---

5   As this book goes on to discuss, being "unique" in the 80s totally sucked. This compares with being unique in the 21st century, which totally smacks of awesomeness.

Flash forward a few years and I was coming up to my ninth year of working in the retail sector in Indonesia. In the midst of this boomtown environment I arrived at a realization that many seasoned marketing professionals still had no idea how to tell a compelling story. What I found most interesting was how personally detached they seemed from what they were selling. It was as if the whole process of issuing press releases and marketing a product was almost a zombie-like pursuit. My experience told me that impassioned storytelling would certainly help make a sale. How was it that people who had been trained to sell to the public had never learned to write or tell a story?

I started hunting for books that might enlighten me on how to teach storytelling to others. Initially, I didn't find any. And so I figured if so few had been written, maybe the world didn't care about the topic. Two years of frustration later, I decided that somebody had to do SOMETHING! So I pulled off my suit to reveal a skin-tight t-shirt emblazoned with the letter 'S' (for Superdry, not Superman), leapt from a phone booth (well, ok, I was just sitting in a chair at the time) and decided to write a book that would guide a new kind of insight into professional and creative storytelling.

And that, my friends, is how my interest in hockey and bookmobiles, and my hatred of cold weather, combined to inspire the upcoming pages that I hope will change the way you look at marketing a product or brand.

The Journey Behind the Journey

"Why is storytelling so important and how can I become a great writer?"

The sad part is that there is no magic formula, just as there is no magic bullet to becoming a great artist, a great singer or a great basketball player. It's really about practice.

However, this book can help you to identify the foundations of becoming a great storyteller. I remember attending a speech by educator and Ashoka Fellow Yohanes Surya. He claimed the secret to improving the education system is to have great teachers teaching great methods and techniques. To prove his theory that anyone could become a math genius, he pulled children out of the poorest villages on the remote island of Papua. He was particularly drawn to students who had failed entire grades or were deemed as "hopeless" by their teachers. In a matter of months, he turned many of them into math geniuses. While his teams have won more than a hundred medals in international science competitions, it is his work in redefining how teachers teach that has attracted global attention.

This book is as much about the psychology of writing stories as it is about the actual storytelling. As Surya so aptly mentions, it's about great teachers and great methods.

The basic premise of this book is that great business stories have, to use rocket ship terms, a pre-launch stage, a countdown stage, a lift-off stage and an orbit stage. In each stage, the art of writing a story involves much more than just simply sitting down and typing. In short, storytelling is much more about basic human psychology than it is about marketing. It's also more than just delivering a pitch. In fact, just as we know the intimate details in the lives of our best friends, it's exactly the same with truly loved brands and products. These brands actually go out of their way to let us know them inside and out while also communicating in the other direction with customers in such a way that they know and relate to the lives of those who use their brand at an intimate level.

In the pre-launch stage, great storytellers formulate the main angle (in journalism talk) of their brand or product's story. To reach that point, it's important to be psychologically on the right page. To get there, I'll address how to move away from thinking about how to satisfy the boss and instead think how to get in tune with your audience. Many marketers operate under an assumption that "if we speak, people will listen". Nothing could be further from the truth. For that reason, this section is less about writing and more about the psychology of stories. Effectively, it's about "how to get your head in the game". After all, how can you let people really know you if you're not prepared to share your story and to relate to them?

In the countdown stage, I'll talk about the concept of "The Journey". In life, in order to be a great friend, you generally need to know all about the other person: where they grew up, what they believe in and what things make them passionate. Products and brands are much the same. Instead of expecting people to love your brand because of what it does, it's important to tell customers how it came into being. This is a new kind of transparent storytelling that I think a lot of marketers miss out on, probably due to classical marketing training grounded in the pre-social media age. In fact, you'll notice that at the beginning of this chapter, the very first thing I discussed was the story of how this book came to be. In this way, I've demonstrated a fundamental premise of journey storytelling.

In the lift-off stage, I'll talk about how to put great stories together, specifically pointing to some technical skills such as developing better wording, alternative story structure and how to manage your hype level.

Finally, I'll talk about the orbit stage. In this stage, your product and brand are already off the ground. However, no story ever really ends. Rather, the best stories are *maintained*. Traditionally, we only thought of stories as press releases and marketing ploys. Everyone knows about tweeting and posting but there are some communication tools that a lot of people fail to see as useful in the maintenance and evolution of your story. Manifestos and apologies that were traditionally seen as internal or reactionary tools can now become a secret weapon thanks to their role in defining how customers see you in an age where information can be found about your product anytime, anywhere.

The ultimate goal of this book is to get you, not so much as a marketer but more as a member of the community of people who connect to your brand or product, to see storytelling in a different way.

I'm a writer by trade, so most of this book will focus on the writing part of the equation. Understanding how to tell your story in a more visual way through packaging, visual merchandising and videos is also very important. I'll leave that to the experts in those fields. That said, while the importance of the written word was diminished for much of the last half-century, writing is making a comeback in a huge way. Thanks to the importance of email, social media and even online dating, becoming an effective and compelling writer is one of the single-most important social skills that a person can possess.

Understanding the skill of storytelling is a work in progress for everyone, including myself. As much as I'm thrilled to be able to share my stories, I can't wait to hear your ideas as well.

TWO

FROM RED SEA TO SHINING SEA

A Brief History of Storytelling

JULES: You know the shows on TV?
VINCENT: I don't watch TV.
JULES: Yes, but you're aware that there's an invention called television, and on that invention they show shows?
VINCENT: Yeah.
JULES: Well, the way they pick the shows on TV is they make one show, and that show's called a pilot. And they show that one show to the people who pick the shows, and on the strength of that one show, they decide if they want to make more shows. Some get accepted and become TV programs, and some don't, and become nothing. She starred in one of the ones that became nothing.

- Pulp Fiction (1994)[6]

---

6 Pulp Fiction. Dir. Quentin Tarantino. Miramax Films, 1994.

Stories have been around since the very beginning of history. Whether you believe in evolution or simply in a higher being (the Bible, Torah, Koran or any other religious book), you've certainly been exposed to stories from an early age. And whether it's the fairy tale of Hansel & Gretel or Santa Claus (possibly the world's most famous commercial story) or the tales of Israelites crossing the Red Sea leaving an army of Egyptian soldiers and their horses behind, some of these stories had a major impact on you. They not only provide you with valuable lessons in life, but they provide context for many other things that you do and become a reference point against which everything is else is measured; an anchor of sorts.

Yet if we look back to more recent history, stories were traditionally not very interesting from a business perspective. While tales of bringing spices from exotic lands were an exception, the need for any kind of story was offset by the simple fact that for a long time, life was just plain difficult for most people. Until the 19th century, practically every task required manual labor and hence buying decisions were either limited (i.e.: you had no choice or had to do it manually) or focused simply around the various functions that the product offered that made your life easier.

Take a historical example. The United States economy in the 19th century grew in large part on the basis of the cotton trade.[7] Planting and harvesting cotton was an exceptionally manpower-intensive and time-consuming task. Because your income effectively depended on being able to afford enough slaves and have enough land, there were really only two factors in play and not much variety or creativity of solutions were needed.

In 1793, Eli Whitney invented the cotton gin and suddenly landowners had an entirely new way to make more money.[8] They could buy fewer slaves, own the same amount of land, buy a cotton gin and immediately make more money. In essence, the cotton gin raised substantially the ceiling on productivity. Cotton gin sellers could simply offer a basic human need (more money for less investment) and make the sale. While a cotton gin was a relatively simple piece of equipment that was hard to improve upon, if you did find a way to do so, certainly you could push the equipment to cotton farmers strictly on function and still make your sale.[9]

---

7   The economy grew on cotton so much so that in 1860, they even fought a big war over it.

8   Even though at first, Whitney and his partners charged a levy of up to 40% of the crop's revenue for each gin they installed.

9   And in fact, many did. Apparently, Whitney's invention and the high cost he placed on it encouraged many people to simply copycat the gin and sell it at a lower price. Since the 1793 Patent Act failed to protect cases like Whitney's, it took him close to 20 years before he was able to get any remedy at all on these pirated items.

The Ultimate Journey

Now if you were a cotton gin salesperson and wanted to tell a story about how the product was invented or how the screws on the gin had been handcrafted in Ireland or England or even in some exotic country like India, people would listen. But in the end, everything would come back to the function and features that your gin was offering. You could tell stories all day and it wouldn't make a bit of difference on whether you would sell any equipment.

This pattern could be repeated over and over in the annals of modern history. Taking a train? Use Baltimore & Ohio Railroad.[10] "We have a schedule and we can get you from Baltimore to Chicago in three weeks." People weren't really interested in stopping for sightseeing, so the story of all the wonderful places you would pass wouldn't really matter. What mattered was that the train arrived at your destination and the price was affordable.

Fast-forward to the days of the Soviet Union (known as the USSR back then). In most towns, there probably wasn't much choice for consumers. If you wanted bread, you joined a long line, chose the only bread available (assuming there was any left), paid your kopeks and left.[11] The bakery could tell you a story about how they were using a rare kind of wheat found only in Ukrainian steppes but that story wouldn't change much your prospect of buying the product. In essence, what mattered was that bread was available and it filled your stomach and those of your family. Function was all that mattered.

The vast majority of purchases went that way because life was generally difficult and many people struggled to make a living.[12] Oh sure, you might buy a horse based on its pedigree or you might visit a show starring the great Harry Houdini who escaped from a straitjacket while perched upside down 50 feet above the New York subway construction zone but those were relative rarities at that time. What mattered for most products was that they filled a very basic human sustenance need through their function and features and cost an amount that was not beyond one's means.

---

10 Which later joined with Central Pacific and Union Pacific to create America's first transcontinental railroad.

11 According to most first-hand and historical accounts I've read, Soviet-era breadlines were not a constant through the entire Communist era. In fact, by all accounts, from the 1950s on, bread was one of the easier items to get and it cost just pennies. Breadlines were apparently more common in the latter days of the Cold War.

12 Considering much of the work was labor-intensive and people back then often lacked basic necessities like electricity, running water and ... the internet.

In the 1950s, we started to see the first examples of true storytelling through the age of advertising. If you watch early advertisements, they were more like mini infomercials with lots of cheesy music and happy smiling faces. Go to YouTube and watch commercials from the 1950s, 60s and even 70s and it's amazing to see how different they are from what we see today.

The post-World War II era was an age of tremendous economic growth in the US and saw the graduation of millions of people into the middle class. Whereas their parents were almost entirely focused on achieving basic sustenance, Baby Boomers were driven by aspirations – a mental picture of what they and their children could be, largely driven by the prominence of a new invention called television. So in a way, the concept of storytelling evolved almost as an outgrowth to higher expectations that typified the post-war era and was amplified by the 24-hours-a-day information cycle that was spawned first by cable TV and later by the internet.

The Golden Age of Storytelling

The larger story with the increase of information flows over the last three decades in particular, and most importantly the last decade, is the emergence of two colliding trends that are making a deeper form storytelling a necessity for business and products.

The first is the trend of "commoditization". If you look at the world today, the barriers to start and copy an existing business model are lower than ever before. There used to be some large barrier, either a lack of information on technical issues, an inability to gather a community without knowing "high-up people" or financial constraints. These ensured that if you had a great business idea, you probably could count on years, if not decades, to build up your name and competitive position before a significant challenger could emerge. At the very least, your product would have needed to be significantly different from that of your competitor in order to "make a dent in the universe".

The television industry is a prime example. In the 1950s, America (and specifically RCA) was the world's pre-eminent maker of TV sets. If you were a Japanese company, nobody in America would trust your quality. As a result, initially the Japanese could compete only by offering lower prices. As the Japanese improved their technology (circa the 1970s and 80s), eventually they overshot the Americans and established a clear technological capability while Korean companies could offer a lower complexity at a lower price. Twenty years later, Japanese companies operated on the higher level of the market but had given away much market share to the Koreans who had nearly the same technology and a lower price, whereas Chinese companies provided lower quality and price.

But there is a catch. The technological and technical gap between where the Chinese are in 2014 with their televisions versus where the Japanese were in the 1950s is staggeringly smaller. In essence, there is not so much to differentiate a Chinese TV today from a Korean one, aside from the brand name and the goodwill that goes along with the name. If you offered someone a choice between a Japanese, Korean or Chinese TV set today, the Japanese brand would have a hard time trying to convince you their product was worth paying a premium of two or three times what the Chinese brand was offering.[13] Perhaps the only argument they could provide wouldn't be so much of an endorsement of their own product, but rather a condemnation of the *perceived* quality of Chinese products. In other words, without a comprehensive story from the Japanese company, the only weapon they have is basically to fill the customer's head with perceived doubts about their competitors.

This repeats itself with respect to pretty much everything we buy these days and even to our own status in life. It was certainly less challenging to "sell" ourselves in a job interview or to other people two decades ago in an environment where there were major differences between our access to education or alternative opportunities and when the global population was closer to 5 billion people as opposed to today's world which is 40% more crowded.[14] As American journalist and author Thomas Friedman so aptly stated, "Average Is Over".[15] Without a truly compelling story, there is now little way for us to differentiate even our own talents, let alone the specialness of products that we are trying to market.

In fact, average is so over that people are going out of their way to be something other than average, searching for experiences in the most unusual places. At one time, we might have looked for experiences only on our vacations, at live events or other special occasions. Today, we seek experiences in everything. To see how much

---

13   And most likely, you would have more like 10 choices from each company, which I'll discuss later in reference to the concept of "The Paradox of Choice".

14   For example, very few foreigners had learned Chinese culture and could run a business in China in the 1980s. Today, the pool is significantly larger. In fact, in 2012, the estimated number of foreigners living in China was close to 600,000 versus 20,000 in 1980. And this is not counting the number of people who had lived and worked in China over the last decade but had left the country since.

15   "Average Is Over" by Thomas Friedman appeared in the op-ed column of the January 24, 2012, edition of the New York Times.

things have changed, one need merely look at an experiment done a few years back where journalist Rob Walker and author Josh Glenn recruited a group of artists to attach a short story to a series of very mundane objects ranging from turkey dinners, lemon velvet bath foam and even a cigarette lighter shaped like a pool ball, and offered them on popular auction sites such as eBay.

How much of a difference did it make? Well, a mini-jar of Hellman's mayonnaise, available at any supermarket for a couple of dollars was given a rather rambling short story by Rick Moody about an encounter on a train with the mayonnaise playfully worked in. It fetched an incredible $51![16] Almost all of the other items used in this experiment saw similar results.

This isn't really all that surprising. When we think of brands in the past, particularly in the luxury segment, products were often sold at multiples of several dozen times the price of comparable products. One big difference from the past is that you can't simply float a simple photo and a brand name out there in order to earn that kind of premium. Another big difference is that the possibility to earn these multiples is not limited to luxury items but can be attached to practically anything these days.

In his book "The Paradox of Choice", psychologist Barry Schwarz talked about the conundrum he faced when going to the supermarket, where he confronted a dizzying array of choices for basic items like breakfast cereal, for which there were 275 options.[17] He went on to discuss the same predicament in dozens of other categories and types of goods ranging from gadgets to suntan oil. Sadly, he's right. The marketplace is very crowded these days.

Prior to reading his book, I related the story in a presentation I did to a group of students of how in many places, having more than 10 choices of bread would have been an oddity even as recently as the 1980s. But in the year 2013, many markets were experiencing an explosion of artisanal bakery chains that offered close to 100

---

16   A full description of the project can be found at significantobjects.com

17   See "The Paradox of Choice" by Barry Schwarz, 2004, Harper Collins, Chapter 1, pp. 8-12. By the way, the average supermarket (excluding big box stores) has an average of 30,000 different choices. You can understand how someone might go into decision overload.

options at any given time.[18] These bakeries would set up trays with small cards telling a small story related to each kind of bread or they might even have a photo of their "Master Baker" (perhaps a photo of some random guy) just to sell the story. Point being, you can't just sell white bread anymore, just as you can't really sell any old leather bag, any old t-shirt or even any old gasoline these days.

The other major trend that happened in the last two decades was what I call the "Democratization of Maven Status". In Malcolm Gladwell's seminal book, "The Tipping Point", he relates how certain trends could explode only if they were powered by certain people who had "stickiness" and kept referring them to others. He used the term "mavens" to describe these people. They were basically "the right kind of people". When mavens say something, people listen.[19]

Of course, for a long time, maven status was limited to only a very few people who appeared in major information spreaders like newspapers, magazines and TV networks. So if you look over the years, you might talk about Oprah Winfrey for consumer products, Gene Siskel and Roger Ebert for movies, Michael Jordan for shoes, radio presenters Dick Clark or Casey Kasem for music or Elizabeth Taylor for style and Craig Claiborne, arguably America's first bona fide restaurant critic. In other cases, mavens took the form of organizations such as the American Automobile Association for hotel ratings or the Better Business Bureau or Consumer Reports. Even at a basic level, we might have used the Yellow Pages and viewed the businesses with the biggest ads as being the most reliable.

How the world has changed!

Thanks to the internet and community-based sites such as Yelp!, Amazon and TripAdvisor and even the use of Twitter and Facebook as centers for ranting and raving, it seems most everyone now has a platform to air an opinion. And while those with the most devoted followings on social media are often celebrities, even previously unknown personalities like Pim Techamuanvivit (Chez Pim – a food blog), Scott Schuman (The Sartorialist – fashion) or Pete Cashmore (Mashable – gadgets and technology) have carved out entire careers founded solely on serving as online

---

18 I used to work in Malaysia, where the default breads that people used to buy came packaged from companies like Gardenia and President's Bakery, firms that dated back decades. But the introduction of bread chains like Bread Talk, Bread Story, Tous Les Jours and dozens of copycats transformed the market into something that even local friends can't comprehend. In fact, it got so bad that one friend went so far as to call the prominent owner of one chain "a crook" for having a share in a bakery that sold bread for about US$5 a loaf whereas the fixed price on a Gardenia loaf would have been about one-fifth of that price. I guess some people's expectations aren't so easy to change.

19 Another word for this is "stickiness", something I'll talk about later.

interactive mavens in their respective areas of expertise. For each of the above bloggers, there are hundreds more who command a wide following.

While the internet and the use of websites and social media have created an avenue for brands to provide a rich storytelling of their own products and services, in many cases, they are missing the opportunity to do so and allowing a whole class of other mavens to dictate their story for them.

An outstanding example of this could be seen in the 2012 US presidential elections. After Mitt Romney won the Republican primaries, President Barack Obama's campaign plunged $65 million into advertising in June, an almost unheard-of strategy among past presidential campaigns, portraying Romney as an unfeeling, inhuman corporate raider. This became the underlying public view of Romney for months until the first presidential debate, by which point enough time and damage had been done that it painted the rest of the campaign culminating in Romney's defeat in November 2012.

The point of this story is that invariably, in the information-driven era of the early 21st century, businesses need to choose who will define their story. If they operate under the same rules as decades or centuries earlier, no matter how much they try to pitch the functionality or value of their product, others will find a more compelling story of their brand. This kind of "message drift" can doom a product, brand or business before it ever has a chance to speak to the contrary.

There is one other aspect to all of this that forms an interesting trend in the information age. As Trendwatching.com pointed out in their 2011 report "Sociallites and Twinsumers", many consumers are now becoming curators of information via social media channels that record their opinions in an effort to brand themselves (referred to by Trendwatching as "Brand Me"). In the process, they gain revered status from readers who find value and their own identity in following these opinions.[20] The consequence of this is that fact and function-based press releases and advertorials that were traditional bedrocks of the marketing communication industry have diminished in importance and have been replaced in importance by compelling stories that can evoke a deeper emotional need in readers.

Again, this comes back to my earlier point whereby function and features don't encourage people to curate as part of their personal brand so much as do stories, uniqueness, shared experiences and emotions that dig much deeper into a person's

---

20 The full article can be found at trendwatching.com/trends/11trends2011

psyche. Therefore, it's fair to say (outside perhaps of Biblical or Renaissance times) there has never been a more important time to share a story.

In that context, storytelling is not so much a skill as a philosophy. It's true that as with anything, the more you write, photograph or video, the more used to storytelling you'll become. But in order to understand how to tell a truly unique story all the time, you need to understand the psychology behind how your readers think and to play off their motivations as opposed to that of your own company. In a sense, just like there has been a focus on bottom-up management with constant feedback mechanisms, so too the best storytelling is built on telling your story *for* the customer instead of *to* them.

PRE-LAUNCH:
THE PSYCHOLOGY
OF FINDING
A GREAT STORY ANGLE

THREE

HOW A HEADACHE BECAME A BRAIN TUMOR

Bringing Your Passion To The Table

LITTLE GIRL: What's the matter?
JOHN KIMBLE: Oh, I have a headache.
LITTLE BOY: It might be a tumor.
JOHN KIMBLE: It's NOT a tumor!! It's not a tumor...at all.

- Kindergarten Cop (1990)[21]

---

21 Kindergarten Cop. Dir. Ivan Reitman. Universal Pictures, 1990.

When I was taking a Dale Carnegie training course as a university student, one of the first lessons we were taught about giving a great public speech was to be passionate and enthusiastic about our subject. [22] Even if you don't have any idea what you're talking about, a little bit of passion goes a long way in this world. In fact, in later years, as part of my job as General Manager of a fashion distribution division, I started to actually ignore resumes and exclusively hire the most passionate people I could find. There's just something about passionate people that allows them to sell sand to the Bedouins or ice to the Eskimos.

In truth, a discussion on passion is important for managers to choose the kind of people who would be good storytellers for their brand. Many CEOs are not classical marketing people and as such they need to hire others to develop stories for them. Sadly, too often we choose people based on their CV as opposed to their personality. This chapter will explain why the person on top of your marketing hierarchy ought to have an innate ability to love your product and communicate it. This chapter is also useful for young marketers in particular as a way of developing their careers in such a way that they can fill this need.

I would like to note as well that when I talk about storytelling, it's not in the context of simply "making stuff up". Truly great storytelling relates to how we recount things that have happened in a way that makes others want to listen. The best stories are the ones that are true.

Mom's the Word

A lot of people don't realize that the first truly great storytellers a lot of us face in our lives are our moms. While the question of whether a maternal instinct to storytell is sociological has proponents on either side of the argument, there may also be a cultural element as well. Classical stereotypes often say that each culture's mothers seem to each have a unique central "fascination". For Italian moms, the joke goes, food is everything. For Chinese mothers, it's supposedly all about making their children study for 39 hours in every 24-hour day. We like to joke that for Jewish moms, it's disease.

The most amazing thing about older Jewish ladies is they can wax lyrical about how people they know are sicker than anyone that the person to whom they are

---

22 In particular, Carnegie was known for his book "How To Win Friends and Influence People" (1936). Over the years, a very notable training course has evolved in teaching people to overcome their fears of meeting new people and public speaking and a range of other interpersonal skills.

talking will ever know. Having the sickest friends is almost like a badge of honor and they have a way of making the story of a close one's illness take on almost legendary proportions.

I was once sitting in a school library listening to our librarian, a stout 50-something classic mother talking to another teacher, an equally portly woman. The conversation was enough to make a 14-year-old cower under a table. It was "The Rumble in the Library"; 15 rounds of Foreman vs. Ali roundhouses about who had the sicker friend. During the course of about 15 traumatic minutes, I swear that the discussion managed to cover at least 11 different types of cancer, explanations of several experimental treatments and I figure perhaps 200 exaggerations of how sick these people actually were.

And yet, the passion of these two older ladies never waned. In fact, they were so passionate that it took two days and a long discussion with my father to tell me that no, I wasn't going to die the next day, before I was able to smile again.

I love my mother with all my heart. She's supremely caring, has sacrificed so much for her family over the years and is a role model for my sister and I on how to always put your absolute best into anything you do in life.

She's also one of the most accomplished and passionate storytellers I know. Whether it's something that she experienced at work or on a trip, the superhuman pace at which my niece and nephew are developing or (every once in a while) the life event of a friend or acquaintance, she is the epitome of passionate storytelling. No matter how many times she tells a given story, she never wavers on her tone, the focus on key things that happened and her key message (i.e.: never fly that airline, my niece and nephew are beyond extraordinary, move back to North America ASAP, etc.). In being so passionate, I can tell you her stories are absolutely compelling. My mom has worked much of her life as an accountant, but had she chosen to be a modern-day marketer, she would have been spectacular at that too.

A Bite of the Apple

One thing that drives a great story is passion. Passionate people tell terrific stories, even about the most mundane products. People who are just doing a job might still be able to sell but people will never become emotionally attached to their product and if they are selling a product that is not inherently exciting (i.e. most products sold in the world), it's likely most of their promotions will focus on low price or discounts.

The above paragraph seems fairly obvious but take a minute to look around the business world. Probably 99% of products out there don't have a definable or interesting story. In a large number of those cases, the people managing those products are probably not particularly passionate about their products.

To get a sense of how something rather ordinary can be made extraordinary by a passionate person, I like to tell the story of a speech by Apple co-founder Steve Wozniak that I once attended. For those not familiar with the Apple story, Steve Jobs was the face of the organization but it was Woz who actually led the creation of a lot of the early Apple products.

Steve Jobs was a marketer. His job was by its nature exciting because he was paid to make everything sound exciting. He was a master marketer, which in turn means he was a master storyteller as well. You couldn't normally get too excited to hear Steve Ballmer or those Blackberry guys get on a stage and tell you about all of these features for their new operating system. But when Steve Jobs took the stage, a lot of the world's population stopped for an hour or so to listen.

Steve Wozniak, on the other hand, was just a techie. For all intents and purposes, you could not imagine a person who had a passion for circuits, chips and software to be able to pull off a truly inspirational speech. And yet there he was, talking in front of 400 people in an auditorium and they were hanging on his every word. He was like a rock star.

He started off with a story about his early years and you could see this was something deeply personal to him. He talked about how his great joy in life since the age of eight was to create things, to get a new electronic machine and pull it apart. Computers were his life. He also talked about the teachers who inspired him and how his father would encourage him every step of the way and gave him every opportunity to advance his life with these machines that he loved so much. I think everyone in the audience thrived off the emotion of that speech and we were all thinking, "That could be me!" He could be talking about how to write Pascal code and we would think it was as exciting as Phineas Fogg's magic flying balloon in "Around the World in 80 Days."

If the programming and electrical engineering professions ever needed a promoter, Woz would be the perfect guy and his life story would inspire a lot of people.

A well-publicized video after the 2012 US presidential election showed Barack Obama speaking to members of his campaign team in the afterglow of their stunning victory. He talked about his own past and how he had been a community organizer fighting for a cause and how the people in that room not only reminded him of himself, but they inspired him. Then he choked up and had to pause while tears rolled down his face. Here was the leader of the free world showing a tint of emotion that was brought out by a pure belief in what he was doing. Obama's passion, grounded in years of community work, was instrumental in raising and maintaining a hardcore base of volunteers who bought into his story. Those volunteers are a big reason why Obama could win two elections.

There is a big difference between writing and speaking when it comes to storytelling. When you tell a story verbally, there are about 1,000 verbal and non-verbal cues that you could communicate - a pause, a quivering voice, a deep breath, looking up at the sky, squinting your eyes, your inflection – that transform your story into a near-odyssey for those listening. People can just "feel" the passion.

Writing is totally different. While storytellers don't have access to the above cues that help sharpen the story, great storytellers have an ability to build context and characters into their story that can make customers "feel" them write. Their vivid descriptions make us close our eyes and travel to the scenario they are describing. In doing so, they create a sense of empathy with these people. That empathy drives the story to a different level. Not coincidentally, after passion, empathy is the other most important character trait that your team must possess.

Finding the Holy Grail of Storytellers

For a company to tell a great story, it's best to start right at the beginning, during the recruitment process.

Very rarely do you find people who adhere 100% to the exact voice and tone of the product and company (more on this later). That said, most great storytellers start with a love of something related to their industry and use that as a launching pad to offset parts of their company's story about which they may feel more neutral or less knowledgeable.

In my own case, despite years of working in the retail fashion industry, people are often surprised to know that I don't like to shop and I don't spend on status symbols. So how could I possibly work in the industry? Well, the simple answer is that I love teaching, training and storytelling. Every product that I've personally chosen to sell has an element of uniqueness and a story behind its design and the way it was made. I love watching people and observing how they act in a group. Doing so has tuned me in to certain aspects of customer experience and their expectations. So while I could learn about the product attributes of handbags, clothes and timepieces, my instinctive ability to understand stories and people, allows me to at least relate my knowledge to my customer.

It's likely that I could have been an even better storyteller if only fashion was my number one interest. Still, because I get such a kick out of helping people, I could still carve out a reasonably successful career as a storyteller in the industry. As I say, it's rare you find the perfect candidate.

How you recruit can be almost as important as who you recruit. For example, The Walt Disney Company is one such company that tries to identify people based on their underlying passion instead of their actual experience. Few who apply for a job in a Disney theme park are aware that even in the reception room, they are being filmed. Disney recruiters ask everyone to fill out an application form before being interviewed yet provide an insufficient number of writing utensils. Everyone in the room has to share with others. If you share, it shows that you have at least some underlying characteristics of friendliness and generosity. If you don't share, you don't even get to the interview stage. In companies like Disney, and especially in a theme park that is the epitome of storytelling from a child's perspective, passion trumps experience.

My best suggestion is that when you interview or evaluate people who might be writing your story, find out if there is some hobby in which they have gotten deeply involved. It could be anything from riding motorcycles to playing sports to traveling the world. Whatever it is, if they can talk about a topic with true emotion and depth, they at least have the potential to tell a story about your product. All that's left is to find that bridge between their own passion and your products, a subject that I'll talk about in depth later in this book.

The key lesson of this chapter is that to be a great storyteller, you need to be a passionate person. If you are passionate about anything in your life, you have the potential to successfully make the leap to become a great storyteller. I'll discuss a bit later how to match your own character with the brand's character to create a great story.

For a great brand to be able to tell its story well, passionate storytellers are a vital prerequisite because most products and brands do not inherently arouse strong emotions in customers. Who writes your story is almost as important as the story itself. Recruiting the right people is key. Once you have the right people, you need to make sure they can connect to their audience. That's where empathy comes in.

FOUR

I FEEL YOU DAWG

Developing the Empathy Superpower

MICKEY: See that picture outside the gym – 'Mighty Mick,' that's me in my prime. I had all the tools. I coulda starched any lightweight husky on the East Coast – But I had no management. Nobody ever got to know how slick I was, but I had a head for business an' stashed a few bucks an' opened the gym – It's a dirt hole, I know it, but that an' a lotta scars is what I got to show for fifty years in the business, kid – now you come along with this shot an' I feel like it's me gettin' the shot I never got ... An' now I got all this knowledge, I wanna give it to ya so I can protect ya an' make sure ya get the best deal ya can! Respect, I always dished ya respect.

- Rocky (1976)[23]

---

23   Rocky. Dir. John G. Avildsen. United Artists, 1976.

Once you have the passion and the passionate people to write your story, the next task is to ensure that you can bring your story to a level that will be relatable to your audience. That's where empathy is important.

Empathy is the ability to understand what another person is feeling. Usually empathy comes from personal experience, the idea that "I've been that guy!" and the "ah-hah!" moment that comes from identifying with the emotions that a person would have encountered in a given situation. Empathy is not just a concept we feel only from a 70s movie about a fighter who feels abandoned by his trainer. There are some extremely poignant real-life applications and examples of how powerful empathy can be.

The Greatest Disaster of All

On December 26, 2004, the Indian Ocean and many of the countries it surrounded experienced one of the worst tragedies in modern times when a 9.0 intensity earthquake rattled the ocean floor resulting in tsunamis that swept over massive areas stretching from Phuket in Thailand to Banda Aceh in Indonesia to Mogadishu in the Horn of Africa. Close to 300,000 people died in the course of a few hours. It was without a doubt, one of the most horrifying disasters imaginable. In Aceh alone, over 200,000 people died, including many family members of some of my colleagues.

On that day, I was in the city of Medan on the northern part of the island of Sumatra (about a 10-hour drive away). At around 7:45 that Sunday morning, there was a rather violent shaking that was felt throughout my hotel. Being a Canadian more accustomed to blizzards and wind chill warnings, I was more than happy to just sleep through it, blissfully unaware that an earthquake of any size is no laughing matter. My traveling companion was shaking me at the time, telling me to run but after quite a long night before, I was pretty happy under the covers and felt that a little "waterbed action" (seriously, that's how it felt to me) was actually quite soothing.

After a few minutes, the shaking stopped. Everything seemed entirely normal. No buildings in Medan seemed disturbed in any way and I figured that the whole thing was "no big deal". Before I came to Asia, I had experienced all of one minor earthquake in my entire life. On the other hand, I once was told that Japanese people have a saying that if the ground is shaking back and forth, you can go about your normal business but if it's shaking up and down, you better run for your life. Well, for me, with my "immense" encyclopedic understanding of earthquakes, I had zero idea what up and down even meant, I just knew "normal" and "something isn't right".

That day, I traveled to the highland towns of Berastagi and Kabanjahe and visited places that I had first experienced years earlier as a backpacker. I actually had a pretty nice day overall.

Even until that night, details of what had happened in Aceh were still fairly sketchy and in passing bus stations with vehicles departing for Aceh, you didn't see any kind of mass mobilization of Acehnese going to visit their relatives. And indeed, because most of the communications in and out of Aceh were completely destroyed by the tsunami, not to mention that many of the most devastated places were buried under water, mud and debris, there wouldn't have been many people to talk with or see anyway.

The next morning, I called my Dad in Canada to wish him a happy birthday and got a steady stream of reprimands from him for not calling earlier. "Didn't you know that there was a massive tsunami near you! We were worried stiff! What the hell were you thinking not calling!" he screamed.

I calmly explained that I really didn't think it was that severe. After all, I had chalked up his worry to the fact that the media has a great way of sensationalizing everything that happens in this part of the world.[24]

I still wasn't entirely sold on the severity of the earthquake, so on my last full day in Medan, I went around the city looking at malls and proceeded on my daily business.[25]

When I returned to Jakarta the next day, the horrific full details of the tsunami were starting to emerge. After the second day, the death toll was expected to be 10,000 people in Aceh. By the fourth day, it had reached 70,000 with many unaccounted for. Days later, the number reached 110,000, then 140,000 before settling at over 200,000. This was a tragedy on a scale that could be felt even

---

24   In my life, I had been around many, many "newsworthy" public disturbances and natural disasters that had been "no big deal". I think to most people it's the exoticness of places like Asia and Africa that makes anything seem possible, so the press seems to find ways to tell stories a lot like my librarian friend in the previous chapter.

25   Interesting story: In the mid-afternoon, I went to a mall which I found was thoroughly unsuitable for the products that I was selling. Nevertheless, I visited the entire mall even up to the top floor just for the sake of being able to say that I had done my due diligence. On the top floor I came across a rather interesting shop selling ringtones for cellular phones and was served by a really friendly sales girl. She seemed extremely engaging to talk to and sold me a ringtone for $1 (which is for me about as big an achievement as selling ice cream to an Eskimo). I invited her for dinner and we sat together for about two hours. Approximately three-and-a-half years later, I married that sales girl.

in a desensitized world like ours where massive tragedies are almost something common.

Images of the suffering were played out on local television 24 hours a day. Despite a three-decade-long insurgency that had resulted in Acehnese trying to secede from Indonesia, just about every Indonesian was glued to their TV and hundreds of thousands rushed out to contribute money through many of the big fundraising efforts that had been set up by local mosques and bigger media networks. Something big was happening; all of the animosity that had been felt over the years disappeared in one fell swoop. It was perhaps one of the great collective awakenings in recent history.

Of course, anyone with a shred of humanity would have contributed to the victims. The Acehnese people had experienced enough misery over 30 years of fighting that a tragedy like this was the horror to end all horrors that they had experienced.

The true measure of this tragedy was laid out in the fact that anyone who saw even two minutes of footage of the disaster could literally feel the pain of these people.

Tsunamis and Storytelling

The reason for me telling the story of the Asian Tsunami is to illustrate the impact of empathy. How people react to events in society can teach us a lot about how we can relate to them in business. Let's examine two possible storylines that could have emerged from that horrible event and see how you feel:

Story #1: "More than 200,000 people died last Sunday as a massive tsunami swept through part of the island of Sumatra. Whole villages were wiped out and major cities are now in ruins."

Story #2: "Imagine what it would be like to lose your entire family in a matter of minutes. Within a blink of an eye, your home might lie in ruins and your entire family washed away."

Do you see the difference? Story #1 actually desensitizes the event with a factual representation that makes you feel that this was something bad but perhaps not something relatable. You could imagine "Joe Smith" sitting on his couch and thinking "Man, that's terrible" and then switching the channel.

Story #2 is quite different. The true story of Aceh lay in the fact that these people lost everything in a matter of minutes. Even after the earthquake hit, there were about 20 minutes where everything seemed ok. The rumbling stopped and, for the most part, buildings were undamaged and few people were injured. If you were a couple of miles from the sea, you would have thought yourself quite safe.

And then BOOM! The water, debris and even drowned bodies rushed in quite from nowhere. If you happened to be on the top floor of your house and your family was downstairs, you could have, in a matter of seconds, been the only person left standing.

Now imagine if you had gone through 30 years of war and economic stagnation. You already had next to nothing materially but could count yourself lucky that at least you had a roof over your head and a family that you could hold on to. The tsunami changed all that.

Think even further how these people would have died. Once a person was swept up in the waves, there was no escape; they were totally left to the unforgiving will of this incredible natural force. In that flood of water, there were a million ways to die, all of them horrific. Think about the old people who had lived through such suffering and didn't have enough strength to hold on for dear life, or even more for those who survived and had no one to take care of them. Or think of the small children or infants who never had a chance to experience life and freedom and love.

Indeed, Story #1 is interesting and notable reading, Story #2 is a horrific tale of suffering that brings you to tears almost to the point that you had experienced it yourself.

That terrible feeling from Story #2 is empathy, and for everyone other than psychopathic personalities, it is a part of our everyday life and the single most powerful emotion that we feel.[26]

It's often said that what separates humans from almost all animals is our ability to reason. I would argue there is something more important, it is our ability feel for others, either our own species or others. When we see others happy or sad or in love or in pain, we somehow manage to pick up on these non-verbal cues and feel for them. We often are afraid of conflict if for nothing else that we're afraid to hurt other people's feelings because if we see them sad, we'll feel sad for them. Sometimes empathy is so strong that our expectation of how we think the other person will feel is stronger than their actual feeling.

---

26 In fact, recent studies show that even psychopaths display empathy. The difference is that the parts of the brain, the insula and cingulate cortex, that control feelings of remorse need to be "activated" instead of just staying switched on like in most normal personalities. There's a good study on this in "Reduced Spontaneous But Relatively Normal Deliberate Vicarious Representations in Psychopathy" by Harma Meffert, Valeria Gazzola, Johan A. den Boer, Amold A.J. Bartels and Christian Keysers in Brain, 2013: 136: 2550-2562.

Putting yourself in another person's shoes is actually so important that one of the lessons that we are taught from very early in life is "Do unto others as you would want done to you," also known as the Golden Rule. It's interesting to note that while every religion in the world seems to find issues with others, practically every group agrees on this single rule. Giving to the poor and caring for other people seems to be an enduring element of every organized religion in the world with very few exceptions.

Sounds great, right? You're probably thinking, "Hey, I didn't spend my money on this book just to be taught the Golden Rule!"

That's true, but in my experience of business storytelling, you would be amazed at how many unseasoned marketers and professionals in general ignore the whole concept of empathy when presenting to audiences. It seems funny that in life we spend a lot of time trying to be considerate toward others but when it comes to selling and promotion, we leave our human feelings, ethics and empathy at the door.

My point is that if you tell your story *to* your audience instead of *for* your audience, people will just turn their heads and ignore it. But if you want to be "invited into their home", you need to tell your story *for* them.

The other thing is that from a business sense, the 21st century is an unrivalled era of choice. Never in human history have people been so overwhelmed with messages and choices as they are now. Whereas as recently as the 1980s, in many countries, people would commonly stand in bread and shoe lines for hours waiting to get their ration for one type of product, this rarely happens anymore. In a free-trade world and a world of cheaply produced products, there are few monopolies left. So as a business, you simply can't think that just because you have a message to share that everyone will listen to you. In fact, if even 2% of your audience is listening to whatever you have to say, you're probably doing a pretty good job.

Most business writers and presenters start from the foundation of what they want to share with people and go from there. If I'm selling computers, I'm going to tell you all about this fast chip and all the cool software you can run off it. If I'm selling clothes, I'm going to tell you how nice and affordable they are. If I'm selling a hamburger, I'll tell you it tastes really good and is made from 100% beef.

By the way, this strategy worked for decades for brands like Commodore, IBM, K-Mart, Levi's, Sears, McDonald's, Burger King and in fact most of the major music labels. You might notice that each of these companies has at one stage or another been in some degree of trouble and seen its market share in its core product decreased or in some cases decimated.

The Ultimate Journey

Empathy allows us to understand what customers really want from our products and brand and gives us an insight into how we can become a valuable friend in their lives. As I talk about "The Journey" later on, empathy becomes a vital ingredient in creating the foundation of your story.

I like to use Apple as an example of empathy. I think what separates Apple's products from others is their ability to understand exactly how users experience products and to anticipate what features we would want or need at any time. In their case, the customer experience is founded on their ability to empathize with their users. After all, the term "customer experience" just means that a company is more attuned to feeling empathy toward its customers.

Avoiding the Fixed Stare Problem

So we've established that empathy is important in creating products and stories that can appeal to certain communities of customers. But here's the problem: About 90% of the marketers I come across do not have any empathy for their customers.

Incidentally this corresponds to the fact that most companies can't tell a story that goes beyond their functions, features and price.

For example, in the retail industry, one of the challenges is that in most segments, products are commoditized enough that it's really hard to make a truly "superior" product. Yes, your product may have some neat functions, but very rarely do you have such an unassailable quality or technical advantage that it couldn't be copied in a matter of days or months by one of your nimble competitors. Many marketers become accustomed to saying why their product is functionally better or priced lower than the competition.

This is a mistake. You would be far better off getting in the mode of talking about why your product solves a customer's basic human need rather than how it simply does a job for them.

I've been working in the watch industry for a while and if you go around, you'll see that there are only so many ways to assemble and present time in a 24 to 48 mm metal case.[27] I could easily talk about leather straps and bracelets and stainless steel types and luminescent hands. Not only is this a way to bore my readers to death, as

---

27 Recent estimates say that more than one billion watches are produced each year. Pretty much anything that could be done has been, several times over in all likelihood.

a marketer, I would get "tuned out" after a while of writing years and years of the same product descriptions.[28]

When I was learning to drive in Canada, instructors would tell us to never look at anything for more than about three seconds at any given time. Even if you looked straight ahead, they would ask you to move your head or take a quick glance at your speed, your rear view mirror, your side mirrors, etc.

It's said that if you look at anything for more than three seconds on the road, you fall into what they call a "fixed stare". At that point, you lose complete track of anything that is happening in front of you, even to the point that you won't notice a car that is careening right at you until it is too late.

Interestingly, in business storytelling and writing, this fixed stare analogy is not so far-fetched. If you write for the same publication or on the same product for long enough, you tend to fall into a habit of doing everything the same way as you did before. If you had developed bad habits and routines and didn't understand how to think from the customer's perspective, it would be as if you were driving in a fixed stare on a deserted country road. Read or listen back to your storytelling and you would find it becoming less coherent and more similar to everything that you had produced before. After a while, it completely loses its impact and you become, well, a dinosaur.

I consider myself a pretty good writer and yet even I've experienced this. I edited a company magazine on luxury watches for close to seven years and by year five, whenever I received an article to edit, I kind of "re-fried it" using the language I thought was best. Interestingly, because I had become so desensitized to the industry, if you read back the writing between my 2009 editions versus my 2006 editions (when I was still new), you could see basically all the same kinds of words and sentence structures being used. I was running out of new things to say.

In the fixed stare analogy, communicators experience a process in which they lose their empathy over time. People want to come along for the ride but they get the same experience time after time after time. Eventually, at least some people will just tune out. Even if your brand and your team start out feeling the lives of your customers, you can still lose it over time. That's exactly when someone else will come along with a better story.

---

28 In fact, after close to six years of editing a watch magazine and reading super boring press releases that have become the industry norm, I nearly did go crazy.

Beating the Inverse 98% Rule

Fortunately, there is a way to avoid falling into a storytelling fixed stare, and that's through starting with and occasionally renewing your sense of empathy. Customers are a living, breathing, ever changing organism. How you tell your story to them will change automatically if you always have that sense of empathy. Brands too need to separate from "selling mode" and use empathy to move into storytelling mode. This is a step up in how you brand your company.

Developing an empathetic view and stepping back from what you have always done is a necessary first step in developing your product or brand's story and it's a skill that remains important even through the orbit stage.

Here's a simple three-step method for bringing empathy back into your brand or your own storytelling style.

<u>Step 1</u>: Clean your mind. Forget what your brands/clients, your product development team and even your boss might be telling you. The general tendency is for the powers that be in your organization to tell you that everything you create is wonderful and people MUST want it. This simply is not true. So if you think like a "company man" you can pretty much forget about being able to achieve empathy.

<u>If you read nothing else in this chapter, please remember this paragraph</u>. For the majority of marketers that I've come across, they subscribe to what I call the "98% Rule". This is to say that they believe that 98% of the world either knows their product and/or brand and more importantly actually cares about it. The reality is that they should be subscribing to the "Inverse 98% Rule" which posits that 98% of the world (or probably more) has little idea of your product or brand and/or *doesn't* care about it (with the majority falling into this latter part). A recent study even went so far as to say that if 70% of the world's brands disappeared, consumers would hardly notice.

As I say, the absolute worst thing you can do is to assume you are "preaching to the converted" because it will bias your entire market approach and only appeal to the tiniest part of the market. The best thing you can do is to feel that you need to actually *earn* the attention of your market with each and every message you send out.

The basic point is to forget everything you've been told about your product. You need to assume that most people are ignorant about you and your product and that your mission is to include them, not to exclude them.

Step 2: Once you've cleaned out your company-based preconception on why you have the next best thing to sliced bread, you need to try to put yourself in the position of your customer. Imagine for a second what they go through in their daily lives. Yes, customer segmentation is a well-known art but what I'm saying here is don't talk about the generalities of your customer demographics. Instead, create a character or think of someone you know who might buy this product and re-trace his or her daily life. What are their hopes? Their aspirations? Their challenges? Their daily activities? Their hobbies? What annoys them? What range of emotions do they go through on a daily basis?

Step 2 is a bit more challenging because we as human beings tend to do this role playing by putting ourselves in the position of that potential customer, not realizing that our own personal experience is biased by our current position ("my product is great" thinking will creep in) and potentially colored by the fact that we are different in our thought process from most other people.

So how do you get that sense of balance in your customer base? These two, used in tandem, are my favorite methods:

1) Think of your own friends and family. Who among this group might be a perfect audience for this?

2) Go on social media and start following strangers who might represent your target market. I mentioned earlier how Malcolm Gladwell talks about "Mavens", those people who influence the actions of a lot of other people. Find some well-known enablers, then follow their friends who think similarly. Twitter is ideal for this as it gives you a fairly detailed picture of an individual's character, likes, dislikes and daily interactions. Find people who tweet a moderate amount.[29]

Focus groups are nice too, but most small and medium sized businesses don't have the money or time to run these so using the "Friends and Family" and "Social Media" routes are great. I love using Twitter because it's a free and easily accessible exchange of information and much less security-constrained than Facebook. If you read 100 or 200 tweets of any individual or follow them for about two or three weeks, you can get to know total strangers surprisingly well. If you ever wanted to know what being a fly on the wall in someone's life is like, follow a random stranger

---

29 It's probably best to avoid those who tweet nonstop as it will make mining for useful data more difficult. I would generally recommend that any profile with between 5,000 and 40,000 tweets would likely be useful. I find people who have between 10,000 and 25,000 tweets to be the most useful.

or even a celebrity on Twitter. You may start to know them better than you know your own friends.[30]

Step 3: Read from different sources. I love resources like Flipboard and Zite because they aggregate content from sources that I might otherwise never see. Reading from these different areas gives me "context" and allows me to fill in the "gray areas" that are kind of unsaid from my individual character profiles and make my observations more universal.

Now that you have started to develop a whole network of "real people" profiles, you can start to put yourself in their shoes, otherwise known as being empathetic.

So again, the amalgam of all of these steps is that *before* you write your story, you need to start asking yourself questions like:

* "What are my potential customers' biggest fears in life?"
* "How could our products impact their lives in a meaningful way?"
* "Why might they actually NOT want to buy my product?"

That last question is a critical one for writing a story. Even after you write your story, you should go back and act like a cynical customer and pick holes in your story just so you can feel what your naysayers may be thinking about you (and believe me, there are probably a lot more of them than you think).

So now what do you do with this empathy? Here's basically where we're leading:

Passion + Empathy = Successful Storytelling

By filling in the left side of the above equation, you and your organization have basically met the pre-conditions for creating great brand stories. The two skills put together give you a roadmap to follow so that you don't get lost along the way.

Now it's time to sync your own personality to your brand so you can reach countdown stage and start crafting the journey for your customers.

---

30 Twitter is such a potent tool for getting "into someone's head" that an algorithm for developing a person's autobiography simply through their tweets is currently under construction by Cornell University Professor Claire Cardie and PhD student Jiwei Li. Entitled "Timeline Generation". The model essentially analyzes different types of tweets and extracts Personal Important Events. The idea being that if the tool is ever fully developed, you would essentially be able to map out your customer's lives on an individual basis without resorting to focus groups or surveys. The great thing about the research is that it applies to the average person. You can view more info on the research in the article by Li "Timeline Generation: Tracking Individuals On Twitter" at arxiv.org/pdf/1309.7313v2.pdf

FIVE

TWO SIDES OF THE SAME COIN

Matching Your Own Inner Voice to Your Brand's Story

ANNIE: I want you to wear these on the road trip when you pitch. (pulling out a pair of red panties)

NUKE: What?

ANNIE: They'll fit snugly against your balls in such a wonderful way that you'll start seeing things differently -- plus they'll remind you of me which is better than thinking about those nasty hitters.

NUKE: Jesus, Annie, I don't know --

ANNIE: You've been pitching out of the wrong side of your brain. These'll help move things to the right side.

NUKE: Big League pitchers don't use these.

ANNIE: They did when they were in the Carolina League.

- Bull Durham (1988)[31]

31   Bull Durham. Dir. Ron Shelton. Orion Pictures, 1988.

For those who have watched "Bull Durham", one of the most unforgettable comedic scenes is that of Nuke, the phenom pitching prospect improving the control of his pitches by wearing women's panties on the mound. It turns out that in baseball, sometimes you can perform better when you think less about what you're doing.

But in writing that's not really the case. If you can't get yourself in the right frame of mind and "think" your way through every word, you can't possibly be a great storyteller.

I talked in the last chapters about passion and empathy. So now let's bring them together and see how you can sync your own character with that of your brand. I mentioned earlier that few people come into a job 100% suited to tell a great brand story. I've boiled down a simple equation that gets you as close as possible to it.

Passion + Empathy = Successful Storytelling

Or in more technical terms:

Inner Voice + Business Voice = Successful Storytelling

Your Inner Voice is basically the "how" and "what" you would write if you were asked to talk about yourself. Let's assume that you were writing an autobiography and could just dictate it (hey, writing isn't for everyone). When you speak to others, place yourself along these lines:

MAP YOUR VOICE

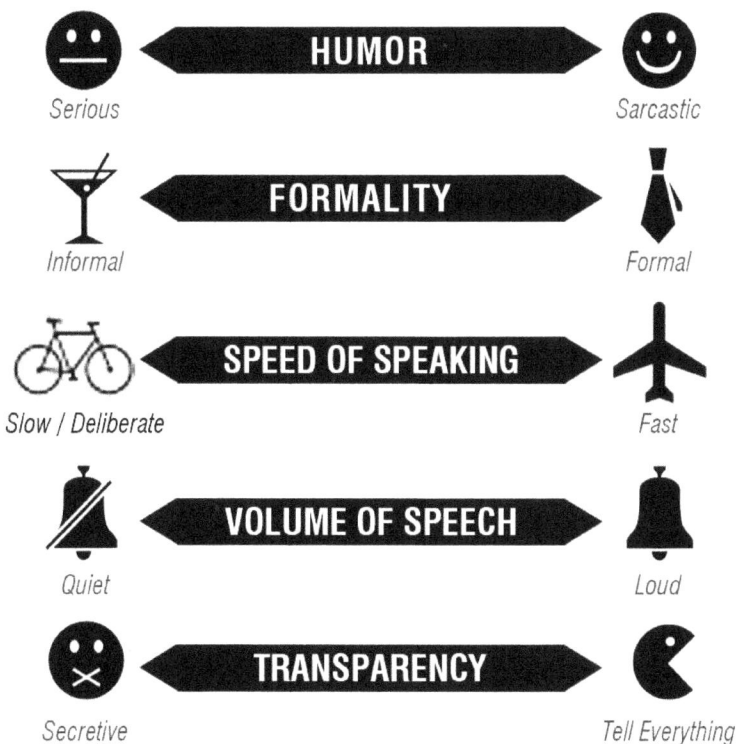

	HUMOR	
Serious		Sarcastic

	FORMALITY	
Informal		Formal

	SPEED OF SPEAKING	
Slow / Deliberate		Fast

	VOLUME OF SPEECH	
Quiet		Loud

	TRANSPARENCY	
Secretive		Tell Everything

Now put two marks where approximately you would sit:

1) When you speak to a total stranger

2) When you speak to good friends

The first mark will be your basic character when you are working on an unfamiliar role. Perhaps it's a 9 to 5 job that you're just taking for the money, or it's good experience but it isn't communicating something about which you're most passionate. Or perhaps this is how you would write about a product that you intrinsically know is not the best in the market. We'll call this your **Passive Inner Voice**.

The second mark will show your basic character when you are working on something you are deeply passionate about, or where you have a vast amount of knowledge. We'll call this your **Active Inner Voice**.

Usually the Passive Inner Voice mark will sit further to the right on the line than the Active one. That's a normal thing. The reason why you plot both of these is that depending on your job, you will naturally adopt one of these storytelling characters as your "default". Unfortunately, as we'll find out later, your default and how a brand wants to talk are not automatically the same. Usually a good brand will ask you to adjust to their character, not the other way around. As writers or storytellers, the better we are at making that adjustment, the more effective we will be. It's really that simple.

This kind of self-identification process is important because in an era of greater transparency, people are expecting brands to speak as if they were actually people or "friends" to whom they can relate. Even years of marketing experience will give you a template that pretty much has to get thrown out the window as soon as you start a new job. Traditional marketing theory has taught us to communicate as salespeople – everything you're selling is communicated as a "must-have" – but in fact to be a great communicator in the 21st century, you ought to adopt the theory that you must *win* the belief of your listeners/readers.

Understanding the gap between your default Inner Voice and that of the brand or product you are representing is the first step to ready yourself to communicate their story. The more passionate you are, the faster you can close that gap. By mapping yourself against your brand, it gives you a constant reminder and frame of reference so that you can always re-focus the tone of your storytelling, even if you accidentally start to drift "off-character" at certain points.

Having said that, let's recap the process. Passion is the building block to ensure you are the right person to tell the story. Empathy is the block that ensures that you can clear the bias out of the stories you are going to write and get on the same page as the customer. The Inner versus Business Voice method identifies how you need to adjust yourself so that your tone and what stories you'll develop will match with your brand and its customers.

In theory, spending three chapters talking about psychology may seem odd. As I said earlier, this is one of the most underrated aspects of storytelling and one most marketers tend to ignore. In reality, the process is neither time consuming nor difficult. Some people can figure this out in an hour while for others it may take a couple of days. In the end, it's a lot like re-learning to walk before you run. In doing so, it will make it so much easier to employ many of the techniques that I'll cover in the upcoming chapters.

COUNTDOWN:
CREATING A JOURNEY

SIX

THE COOKIE MONSTER, THE MAHARAJA AND THE PRESIDENT

Bringing People on "The Journey"

DEAN (TV Shopping Channel Host): You're goin' to that seniors' cocktail party? It's bingo night and you're lookin' for somethin' to wear? How about a 13-carat panzoto-panzanite ring. This is-oh! We got a caller already on this one! Hello sir, you must be a fan of panzoto-panzanite.

STAN: Yeah, hi. Um, you should kill yourself?

DEAN: ...What's that?

STAN: I said, you should kill yourself. What you do is sort of, unjustifiable. And you know it's unjustifiable. And you don't care. You're the definition of evil. Kill yourself.

DEAN: Ok, we're gonna sell this ring for just thirty-seven ninety-five. How's that?

STAN: I just read that the day shopping networks make most of their money is on the day seniors pick up Social Security checks. Kill yourself.

DEAN: Alright, well you shouldn't say things like that 'cause... some host of a jewelry channel sure might up and do it, and then you'd feel really bad.
STAN: No I wouldn't.

- South Park "Cash For Gold" (2012)[32]

32 "Cash For Gold." South Park. Comedy Network, March 21, 2012. Television.

The Ultimate Journey

The preceding exchange is from a great South Park episode about TV shopping channels selling jewelry to pensioners who couldn't afford it. While real home shopping networks like QVC are not nearly so nefarious as depicted in the episode (although they probably don't help adult obesity or savings rates very much), there is much to be learned from how they sell.

Consider that until the creation of QVC and other networks (or even infomercials), storytelling from a distance was very much a lost art. Sure, mail circulars were commonly used in the 70s, 80s and even 90s to let people know about things that were not available within physical proximity to them, but all of this storytelling was pretty much two-dimensional, consisting of words on paper. It was only with the creation of home shopping networks and infomercials that delivering storytelling became a three-dimensional affair, including the creation of special lines of jewelry and clothes, often with the participation of celebrities, where there was a true mosaic behind how the product had been created and its varied benefits. If old clichés like "seeing is believing" or "a picture can speak a thousand words" seemed fitting, it's because the confluence of sight, sound, words and limited time discounts or limited stock created something that really took the art out of the box.

If we look closer, networks like QVC in a sense provided a catalyst for developing a new method of storytelling that I call "The Journey".

Where Did Journey Storytelling Come From

As mentioned earlier, prior to the age of mass distribution of consumer products in the 18th and 19th centuries, selling was a highly personal affair. Proprietors of stores lived in the same community as their customers and products were generally conceived, grown and marketed in the same area as where they were sold. Brands were very rarely faceless in that customers had complete transparency about all aspects of the story of what they bought.

The invention of motorized transportation such as trains, automobiles and airplanes set off a domino effect in the 19th and 20th centuries causing an increasingly significant distance to form between brand owners and their customers. The creation of national and international brands began a process whereby marketing and promotion became a question of awareness much more than the actual quality or identity of the products and who owned them. As many brands became public entities, consumers became less aware of the products they were buying even as they were becoming aware of a larger quantity of faceless brands and products via television, radio and movies. Often times, brands might ask celebrities to provide them a representative face. In many cases, this resulted in brands taking the identity of their endorser rather than creating their own story.

In the past, consumers could only contact companies using relatively expensive phone calls[33] or through the slow process of snail mail. Consequently, it was actually rather costly and time-consuming to find out more information about a brand or product beyond what was being advertised.

The internet age has changed that and now customers are looking for brands to share more of their identity, not less. This is where the concept of a journey can play an important role in creating a new type of perception of a brand or product formed entirely around a larger story.

What is a Journey?

As with any vacation we take, the concept of a journey is founded upon a few basic elements:

1) **The Idea**: Usually we take a vacation based on a certain human need. Perhaps we are stressed out at work or maybe it was aroused by a book, TV show or movie that we saw. For storytelling purposes, the idea originates from a person or a group of people who experienced something that compelled them to act and create a new product to fill a need.

2) **The Process:** Just as we book a ticket and pack for our trip, a business story evolves through a process of trial and error in designing the product including the reasons for its functions, sourcing it, the process of transporting it, marketing it and so on.

3) **The End Product:** Just as getting on the plane is a climax, so too is the final product. It's kind of like "here's what we came up with".

4) **The Awesome Event** (optional): Usually when we go on a vacation, it's made great by some unexpected yet very happy thing that happened to us. Perhaps we met a new friend, got a free room upgrade or accidentally wandered to an amazing place. For business storytellers, the awesome event happens when people start using our products or brands and experience something great. Maybe

---

33 People often forget that as recently as the mid-1990s it could cost $0.35 per minute or more just to call to a different area code within the same city using the purchasing power of that time. That was up to 10% of an hourly wage for many people. Today, a Skype call halfway around the world costs less than $0.02.

it's the happy customer who was able to visit their family for the holidays for the first time in ages, perhaps it's someone famous starting to use our product because they just loved it or maybe it's a case where our brand or product helped out a community in some way.

This flow of storytelling begins when introducing your brand to the public for the first time. This is where you talk about your founders, the origin of the product idea, how you brought it to market and of course what it does. This would also be a great time to introduce your manifesto, assuming you have one (I'll talk about manifestos later).

After this first round of storytelling is done, as and when you launch major product lines, your story can switch to focus on those products effectively using the same four-step process as per above: Where did the product idea come from? What were the challenges and design considerations in creating it? What does it do and how is it special?

The goal of taking customers along for a journey is that they develop a unique emotional bond with your brand and your product. By being transparent, you are welcoming them to become almost an extension of your company. This is an entirely new kind of relationship that can be shared through videos but also specifically through written communications on your website, press releases, social media, internal and external newsletters and even on packaging.

In order to better understand the concept of journey storytelling, I would like to tell the story of the late Dave Nichol, a man who single-handedly changed how people saw private label brands forever.

A People's Revolt: The President's Choice

The present-day supermarket is actually a relatively new invention. Created in the early 19th century by the Great Atlantic & Pacific Tea Company (also known as A&P) to take advantage of growing urban communities that lived far from a fresh food source, supermarkets went through a number of iterations over the years. Beginning as glorified general stores, they evolved first to self-serve formats (started in 1916 by Piggly Wiggly in Tennessee) where people could actually touch products for the first time, to eventually achieving the modern format we know today (there's some debate which was the first but many claim it was Ye Market Place in Glendale, California, in 1924) that provided a combination of national brands, fresh meat and dairy and offered free parking to the newly automotive-crazy society.

The initial supermarket chains would have carried anywhere between 600 to 1,100 items (also known as SKUs or store keeping units). As an illustration of how much the modern-day supermarket has grown, in 2010 the average number of SKUs in a standard supermarket numbered around 38,000. Of course, you would have more SKUs in today's world given that the average supermarket is also approximately 34 times larger than the original incarnation.

By the 1980s and early 1990s, the industry roost was ruled by a few select suppliers. It was estimated that six firms (Cargill, Unilever, Kraft/General Foods, Nabisco, Proctor & Gamble and ConAgra) controlled close to 67% of all supermarket sales in 1993. And in an interesting twist, most category leaders from as early as 1925 remained as such in 1985. So if a Piggly Wiggly in 1925 was dependent on Kellogg cereals, Colgate toothpaste or Coca-Cola, you could time travel to six decades later, you would find that these same brands still controlled the shelves, and by proxy, the supermarket themselves. Suppliers could effectively lock out any supermarket daring to defy conventional wisdom.

The same phenomena could be observed in other industries. A watch store that does not sell Rolex watches would have trouble surviving in today's world. So too for a movie theatre that was locked out of the rights to the latest blockbusters from any of the largest studios, a tire shop that supplied none of Michelin, Goodyear or Bridgestone or a phone shop that wouldn't be supplied by Samsung or Apple. Not having these category leaders could degrade your store to the ranks of the "minor leagues".

Still, having a category leader was no guarantee of achieving profitability. On the contrary, it was very nearly the opposite. Most supermarkets in the 1980s would average a gross margin of approximately 30% across the board but on category leaders might actually offer their best selling products *below* cost. Invariably, it was only the brands themselves that benefitted from such competition.[34]

Canadian supermarket chain Loblaws was just one of those many competitors and they operated a number of different concepts even down to a store chain called No Frills which really was just that. It offered name brands at low prices but was partly focused on its own house brand of products of the same name in simple yel-

---

34 The same is true today. In my own industry, the watch wholesale industry, Ma and Pa shops locked in fierce price competition on the largest brands tended to sell them at a margin of less than 5% whereas the standard discount might have been 30-40% off regular price. This was not enough to cover the cost of unsold inventory and resulted in significant credit crunches for many dealers.

low packaging. Although the company was part of one of the country's largest food conglomerates, the Weston Group, it struggled financially.

No Frills was a good concept for those looking to save money every day but wasn't the kind of place you could fall in love with as it was as non-descript as any other supermarket. The No Frills products were not any better than branded products, just cheaper, very much like generic drugs versus their brand name counterparts.

Enter Dave Nichol ...

Nichol was born in Canada and was a graduate of the prestigious University of Western Ontario Business School where he came to meet Galen Weston, a member of the family that owned the Loblaws chain. In 1972, Nichol joined Loblaws as an Executive Vice-President and was promoted to President in 1976. During the 1970s, Loblaw's tried to develop a number of store brands under the names No Name, No Frills, Too Good to Be True, and Green. While the brands generally performed adequately, none really took off. Similarly, all of the chains operated in an environment of tight margins and little differentiation. People pretty much shopped wherever they got the lowest prices.

In 1983, while scouting for new products for its No Name brand, Nichol worked against the market to create a new premium quality of packaged coffee, at a time when leading coffee brands were actually reducing the proportion of Arabica beans in their blends (this trend was one of the justifications for Howard Schultz to take over Starbucks in 1979). The coffee hit Loblaws' shelves during Christmas 1983 and instantly became the top-selling item in the stores.[35]

Nichol recognized from this that there was a certain place in the market for customers to trade up in store brand products and started creating a whole line of products under the President's Choice banner. Nichol's underlying goal in every product was to offer a premium product that was better than the major national brands, yet could be offered at a reasonable price. In many cases, Nichol spent his time creating products and categories that were not even widely available in the market, ranging from cookies to drinks to hamburgers to sauces and other condiments.

---

35 The most complete story of Dave Nichol and the development of the President's Choice brand can be found in "The Edible Man: President's Choice & the Making of Popular Taste" by Anne Kingston, published by Macfarlane Walter & Ross, 1994. Many of the insider accounts in this chapter related to the development of The Decadent are taken from that book.

Had Nichol simply created the brand just to produce products, President's Choice might have eventually become a successful brand but would never have become a global brand in itself. It required communication.

But First a Step Back...

Dave Nichol was not the first person to develop a supermarket based on in-house products. In 1958, California native and Stanford graduate Joe Coulombe developed a chain of Los Angeles-based convenience stores known as Pronto Market. The Pronto Market was a merger between the drug store of the time and a food market, and was founded on his experience with drug company Rexall. The entry of Dallas-based 7-Eleven to the Los Angeles market in the 1960s forced Coulombe to rethink his strategy and in 1967, Coulombe opened the first Trader Joe's supermarket on Arroyo Parkway in Pasadena, California.

Coulombe's introduction to 'exotic' foods and ingredients came from a fellow student Alice Steere, the daughter of a Stanford professor. A dinner invitation to her house was the first time, Coulombe had ever tasted olive oil. His new concept targeted sophisticated shoppers, merging a more refined version of a liquor store with his existing convenience store concept.

Further reading (apparently from Scientific America magazines) also convinced him of the major changes in the earth's environment and encouraged him to take a "green" view on his product development at a time when the environmental scene was very much in its infancy. The arrival of the Boeing 747 jumbo jet, making transcontinental travel affordable for more than just the most elite members of society, ushered in an era where not only would such a sophisticated market focus on a range of American products, but one in which their tastes would be influenced increasingly by non-American flavors, few of which were available in the traditional supermarket.

As the Trader Joe's concept developed in the 1970s, Coulombe developed this unique combination of fine ingredients, environmentally-friendly, healthier and ethnic products and a store concept that focused on only 5,000 or so SKUs, with only a couple of choices in each category. By focusing on his own lines of products with an aesthetic and fairly uniform packaging, Coulombe was able to guide visitors on a kind of accessible journey through his stores. Even today, Trader Joe's generates higher revenue per square foot than either Whole Foods or Wal-Mart.

The Ultimate Journey

Perhaps what made Coulombe the original master of the supermarket was his storytelling ability. In the 1970s, as an effort to educate his customers on the value behind his proprietary products, Coulombe developed a small circular which he called "Insider's Report". Coulombe's circulations were a mix between comic book and consumer report on products ranging from copper cookware to Kiss My Face olive oil soap.

On one trip to California, Nichol came across the Insider's Report. In 1983, he purchased the rights to the name and the concept from Coulombe for $25,000.

Meet the Maharaja

In 1984, Nichol started publishing his new Insider's Report, which he described as "a cross between Mad Magazine and Consumer Reports". The report extended to 30-minute infomercials with Nichol being the chief spokesperson (a lot like Steve Jobs would become later) but far and away the most anticipated communication came in the form of the printed circular that was inserted every quarter in the Saturday edition of newspapers like The Toronto Star.

The magazine featured a photo of Nichol and his bulldog, Georgie Girl, on the cover with comic-like stories describing the new products for that season. The Insider's Report was different in that it not only described the various benefits and unique qualities of each product but went beyond to also describe the story of how Nichol and his team had come across the product and they had personally led to its development in the hopes of creating the finest in its class.

I remember from my childhood that these stories made me a fan of the President's Choice brand. It was so fascinating that I would never fail to read the Insider's Report from cover to cover. The stories not only made the products sound delicious but also transformed them into this incredible story of discovery, kind of like an eccentric uncle telling his enthusiastic nephew or niece of his latest adventure overseas.

Take, for example, the Memories of Jaipur curry sauce that become one of the brand's favorite cooking sauces:

"While staying at the Rambagh Hotel in Jaipur, India (the former home to the famous polo-player Majaraja of Jaipur), we were served shrimp grilled with a sweet and sour curry sauce that surpassed every curry dish we had tasted before. The sauce from the Maharaja's kitchen wasn't easy to duplicate but after many attempts we finally discov-

ered its mouth-watering secret and bottled it as President's Choice. This delectable curry sauce is best mixed with rice or as a spicy sauce or glaze for meat, poultry or seafood."[36]

The Decadent

Creating a superior chocolate chip cookie was long a target of the company since the introduction of the original President's Choice products. Nichol confidante Jim White, a former Toronto food writer who became chief storyteller for the brand, claimed prior to being hired that the ultimate chocolate chip cookie was one of the 100 largest "hook" products that the brand could make. At the time, the category was entirely dominated by Nabisco, particularly through its best selling Chips Ahoy! cookies. The barriers to entry were significant.

The company had worked over time on its cookie competency and in 1987 put out a competitor product to Oreos called Lucullan Delights. I tried this cookie when I was younger. It was excellent. But it did not blow me away. Little did I know that the following year something great was coming.

In April 1988, Nichol and President's Choice released The Decadent Chocolate Chip Cookie, a cookie that contained an astonishing 40% of its weight in chocolate chips (the cookies were really, *really* good!). Finished with a slightly browned topping, a coconut aftertaste, real butter, the star of the cookie was chocolate that was kept at sub-zero temperatures until just before baking.

At that time, a cookie that contained 40% of its weight in chocolate chips was probably not the most desirable product since it emerged just as the whole weight loss trend was kicking into high gear. While the packaging was impressive (a tasty-looking glob of chocolate chips with one solitary cookie in the foreground), it was this incredible story of trial and error to create the ultimate chocolaty treat that really captured the imagination of the public. Pretty soon, The Decadent cookies were not just a hit in Canada but were being sold in a handful of other countries as well. While other brands like Chips Ahoy! and Oreos could counter with products that tried to match the 40% ratio, they quickly lost considerable market share to The Decadent. In just six years, Nichol managed to sell close to 1.2 billion cookies, more than 47 million packages.

The success of The Decadent, Memories of Jaipur and countless other products has as much to do about the storytelling of the Insider's Reports as it does the

---

36 Insider's Report, June 20, 1993.

product, the packaging or the merchandising. The fact that the development of nearly every product was made quite public via the Insider's Report added an extra dimension of adventure for a large niche of customers looking for a unique taste and culinary experience. This allowed these relatively commonplace products to leap past well-established competition. In the end, great storytelling played a big part in this.

One lesson behind the development of The Decadent is that the only way to write a great story about a product is to have the story in mind when you make the product, as opposed to writing the story after the product comes out. In the case of The Decadent, the hook was to create a product that was undeniably different from other cookies on the market, so that the story would tell itself. Merely having 40% of a cookie composed of chocolate was unheard of. Invariably, the chocolate chips would tell the story.

When Nichol described the story of The Decadent with a huge plug on the front page of his April 1988 Insider's Report, he capitalized on the use of superlatives. "In my opinion," Nichol proclaimed, "these are the best food product we've ever created!" When a trusted consumer advocate claims in the first person that he would choose this product over any other, that's an endorsement that is sure to be heard.

But what helped just as much was that the Insider's Report detailed the trials and tribulations of testing multiple suppliers to make the cookie until he found Colonial Cookies, a company in nearby Kitchener, Canada that was able to perfect the taste. This set the stage to create an even greater relationship with customers and translated into hundreds of successful product launches thereafter for the President's Choice brand. No customer could ever doubt that Dave Nichol would go to the ends of the earth to find the best products for them.

The President's Journey

From the example above, we could see the concept of the journey done time and time again from the inception of the idea through to the end product. In the early days, Nichol became the company spokesperson, talking about his idea for the President's Choice brand and establishing credibility through his singular focus on premium and exotic products at prices below the national brands. Every time he launched a new product like a curry sauce or a cookie, he would talk about why he came up with the idea for the product, where he found it, how they designed it and then about why it's amazing compared to anything else in the market. President's Choice customers were taken for journey after journey after journey and, based on the business results, loved every minute of it.

Sometimes brands or products have a story that can go beyond the first three steps and gain special traction on that fourth step, the awesome event. TOMS is one such brand.

A Shoe on the Other Foot

TOMS is a California-based fashion company started by serial entrepreneur and former The Amazing Race contestant Blake Mycoskie. If you meet Blake in person, he's the epitome of the ultimate salesperson. He speaks in an excited tone about just about everything and there's sincerity in his eyes that you simply can't ignore. The fascinating Texas to Argentina to California to the world journey that is part and parcel of the company's history forms a vital link that has made the brand one of the most loved in the world.

Blake started TOMS after a backpack trip to Argentina, where he met some volunteers who would bring shoes to villages for children who were too poor to afford them. He was inspired by the trip to do something even bigger and managed to turn an Argentinian country shoe, the *Alpergado*, into a must-have item for anyone who wears a pair of shoes, albeit one with a very special mission.

Blake well understood that people do not get very excited about just any new brand of shoes. Shoe brands come and go depending on the season, the style and the price. What really got people excited about TOMS was the "One For One Promise", a simple yet elegant commitment to donate one pair of shoes to the poor for every pair sold. All of a sudden, people discovered that not only could they buy a pair of shoes, they could also be part of a larger mission.

Over time, Blake and TOMS promoted their shoe drops, giving trips in which people signed up to visit remote villages and physically hand over shoes to these poor children. As a wise person once said, "the only time volunteerism really works is when the volunteer does it for themselves, rather than just the people they're helping." TOMS story went from being about a simple pair of $65 shoes to something where people could be part of something greater than themselves.

The TOMS story is the epitome of a journey, much like the great journeys that the late Dave Nichol talked about when he was creating those terrific President's

Choice products. Blake's backpack trip and his epiphany are as much a part of the story as One For One.[37] Not only do you have a great product, you have this incredible story about small villages in Argentina that led to the creation of the brand.

Second, the TOMS brand was started out of a greater mission than simply to sell a product. Because it was founded on the basis of "changing the world", it demonstrates the power of empathy to a tee. People can relate to the happiness that a child might feel when receiving a new pair of shoes. They can relate to the idea that TOMS are made by decent people who want to leave something good in the world. Furthermore, people who went on shoe drops talked about these incredible visits to foreign lands and the people they met and affected. This is the distinguishing "fourth step" of the journey, the awesome event.

Subsequently, as TOMS launched new products like eyewear, they repeated the same journey story as with shoes, explaining the idea to launch eyewear, how they created a One for One proposition for that product and the visits to do operations and provide free eyewear to those in need.[38]

Taking a Cue from the Music Industry

For decades, anyone with their hand on the pulse of the music-listening community would know that most people absolutely *hated* shelling out $10-$20 for an entire tape, record or CD with 11 songs, 10 of which they didn't care to listen to. On top of that, people couldn't be bothered to carry a hundred CDs or tapes with them everywhere they went. The music companies' message: "We have this amazing new song out, now you can buy it on Artist X's new album! Available in record stores now!! Oh, and while you're at it, make sure to buy Artist Y's and Artist Z's and Artist A's thru W's albums too!"

In the early part of this century, Apple had another idea. What if you could hold just the songs *you* wanted to hear in the palm of your hand? And *you* could have the freedom to buy whatever songs *you* wanted for just a small fee. And imagine if we could give *you* a tiny device that you can bring *anywhere* that could hold hundreds of your favorite songs. Imagine how amazing that would be *for you!*"

---

37 If you read Blake Mycoskie's book "Start Something That Matters", it's a spectacular review of not only the TOMS story and the journey from backpack trip to powerhouse brand but also of the whole concept of incorporating giving into your business model.

38 TOMS is one of the best brands I've seen for maintaining the journey of their brand. They have an entire section on their website called Stories. You can find it at www.toms.com/stories

The average music fan took a while to wake up to this but when they did, you could hear a collective "Screw you, miserable greedy music executive! I want my freedom!"

That little piece of equipment was the iPod and it changed the way we listen to music forever!

Steve Jobs and his team at Apple felt people's pain. Yes, they wanted to make money but they had the ability to empathize with the average person. And everything they wrote and presented was done in that way.

Here's how Moby presented the iPod at the company's first presentation on the new device back in 2001:

> *"I've had three MP3 players and I haven't figured out how to use any of them. And this one, I held it and 45 seconds later, I knew how to use it. I'm having a hard time getting my head around that you can transfer an album onto this in 10 seconds. If I was 16 years old, I think I could deal with that a lot better."*[39]

In fact, this story is so simple – easy to use, de-mystifying, mind-blowing and not just for teenagers. In 20 seconds, they debunked the fears that millions of people were feeling. They took technology and made it human.

Flash forward a few years later and Apple produced a commercial to explain their newest invention, the iPad, which had nothing to do with features. In that commercial, entitled "We Believe", it talked about freedom and power, two universally pursued goals of just about everybody. The iPad resonated with people too and the rest, as they say, is history.[40]

Notice again, Steve Jobs was already known for creating amazing desktops. People already knew and trusted him, the Apple name and what both stood for. The iPod introduced by Jobs related to a specific need that he identified, with a full explanation of all the design considerations and with special note to how it would change people's lives and the music industry in general. Moby's voice only sounded out what most people were thinking when they got their first iPod. The journey had propelled the iPod from a mere music player to a must-have item.

---

39   You can watch it at www.youtube.com/watch?v=tfOciT044zE
40   You can find the commercial at www.youtube.com/watch?v=EblcnLuBM7A

Bring It On

Notice also that real names were used. Dave Nichol, Blake Mycoskie and Steve Jobs are real people, not hidden corporate leaders. Great journeys are always about the people you get to meet. We'll talk in the next chapter about just how important those people can be. Each story invoked a process for designing the best product and building a movement of believers. Each story talks not only about function but how those functions solve a need that was the basis for creating the product. In some cases, there's a follow-up involving experiences of how the product or brand had created an awesome event, changing the lives of certain people who had touched the product.

In sum, bringing your customer through the entire process of product creation, including all the challenges that went into getting it just right and the impact it has on society as a whole, provides an emotional insight that can be really hard to beat. Rather than just selling a product, writing and exposing the journey is like bringing the customer "along for the ride". Anyone who has ever gone on a road trip with their friends or worked on a hard project with a small group of teammates can tell you that shared experiences create the strongest bonds. These experiences make for lifetime relationships. Isn't this what every brand can only hope for?

SEVEN

THIS PRODUCT IS 100% GUARANTEED TO LEAD TO DIVORCE OR YOUR MONEY BACK!

Putting a Human Face to Your Journey

AL CAPONE: Life goes on. A man becomes pre-eminent, he's expected to have enthusiasms. Enthusiasms ... Enthusiasms ... What are mine? What draws my admiration? What is that which gives me joy?
Baseball!
A man stands alone at the plate. This is the time for what? For individual achievement. There he stands alone. But in the field, what? Part of a team. Teamwork Looks, throws, catches, hustles - part of one big team. Bats himself the live-long day, Babe Ruth, Ty Cobb, and so on. If his team don't field ... what is he? You follow me? No one! Sunny day, the stands are full of fans. What does he have to say? "I'm goin' out there for myself. But ... I get nowhere unless the team wins."

- The Untouchables (1987)[41]

---

41   The Untouchables. Dir. Brian De Palma. Paramount Pictures, 1987.

In "The Untouchables", Al Capone sends a rather precise message to one particular partner whom he caught ratting him out to the police. Shortly after this speech, Capone takes the baseball bat and smashes the skull of the perpetrator with a single blow to the back of the head. Blood spills all around and gasps are heard from everyone.

… And CUT!

I love this quote. It's one of my favorites in all of movie history because it's so true. There are times in life and in business when we act for ourselves. There are other times when we can't succeed without the help of a team. It's a long way from the old Budweiser "Leon" beer commercial where a sports reporter is interviewing a star player, who is constantly blaming his teammates for their loss, to which the reporter sarcastically quips, "There's no 'I' in team."[42]

The social media generation has heralded in an era where individual achievement and teamwork are almost enmeshed in an inextricably woven patchwork. In fact, if one person really achieves, the whole team can win. Sometimes, it's better for a company to use the voice of "the average guy" rather than speaking as a corporate voice or "renting" a celebrity. Creating a face of the company who isn't a corporate leader but rather is just an ordinary guy is an extremely unique and powerful way of taking people on a journey.

And this partly explains the supremacy of one specific gaming company that toppled an industry giant.

It's More Than a Game: The Story of Ronnie2K and 2K Sports

It was said that the era of the video game was at its apex in the 1980s. Anyone who remembers playing games on the first Atari or Nintendo systems (or any computer for that matter) would remember such titles as Tetris, Space Invaders, Donkey Kong or the two "giants" of the video game world, Pac Man and Mario Brothers.[43]

If you were growing up in the 1980s, you would probably have spent insane amounts of time and perhaps even partly viewed your own life's success on what

---

42 By the way, Leon's response is classic. "There ain't no 'we' either." I want to find the scriptwriter of that commercial and hug him or her.

43 It may be hard to imagine but at that time, "handheld" electronic gaming devices could be used to play only one game. You could imagine that your travel bag for trips would have been pretty full. Well, it's a long way from Gameboy, that's for sure.

level or what score you had achieved in any or all of these games. Invariably, there's something deeply engrossing and addictive about video games, particularly among guys. Perhaps it's our innate *alpha male* desire to shoot at stuff or "kill the largest woolly mammoth". Whatever it is, it cannot be understated that you could not disturb a guy when he was about to win a game of Super Mario Brothers.

In the early 1990s, video games sort of went by the wayside. Perhaps it was because they had become a bit passé, perhaps the world was first getting used to the wonders of the internet. People still played video games and some innovations were happening including the use of 3-D, but the industry stagnated to a large extent.

In the early part of the new century, video games started to make a comeback. Led by realistic games that actually encompassed a whole script, such as Grand Theft Auto, the video game industry experienced something of a renaissance. Now, not only could you challenge yourself to finish a game, but also you could compete online in real time with other people around the world and promote your successes via social media and through online forums.

Grand Theft Auto and similar titles brought the strengths of movies through glorification of violence, drugs and prostitution to the video game screen. Yet, at the same time, another genre of video games started to emerge that appealed to a different type of audience, the sports fan.

For someone who grew up playing sports simulation games like Strat-O-Matic and Pursue the Pennant, the ability of video games to more accurately simulate the real sport was a great leap forward from the use of dice or complicated player cards. Although Electronic Arts was initially the master of the genre, over the years, another upstart company based in the Bay Area, 2K Games, started to make strides toward breaking that dominance and created a story that took the world by storm.

The company was founded in 2005 and purchased many of the Sega franchise games including the "NBA 2K" series that had first appeared in 1999. Over the years, the company has diversified the series, adding celebrity announcers, making the simulations even more lifelike and expanding the number of devices on which it can be played until now you can even play their games on a tablet.

Today's NBA 2K (and the games that followed it, including licenses from the NHL and the WWE) are, to my knowledge, THE most life-like sports games I've ever played. Even the simple mobile version, although more limited than the versions available for gaming consoles, has such incredibly realistic strategic elements to what actually happens in basketball, even down to the various ways of dunking or shooting, that playing the game feels a lot like watching the NBA on TV. At times, I actually have to re-adjust my mind a bit for the first couple of minutes I watch a real game so that I don't get confused with my video game perceptions.

The Face of the Franchise

For all its functional superiority, the story of 2K Games and 2K Sports has taken on an entirely different life since the hiring of current Digital Marketing Director, Ronnie Singh, known to many in the social media universe as @Ronnie2K. What he has been able to do in crafting a story that has spread like wildfire using his own personality is a textbook illustration of how inserting a person into the position of corporate storyteller can make a story absolutely burst into life and shows the incredible power of the concept of "relatability".

According to Ronnie, a self-proclaimed sports addict, his progression to the field of corporate storytelling and current standing as the "Face of the Franchise" happened by chance as much as anything. After graduating from the University of California in San Diego, he went on to work with the independent professional Golden Baseball League's San Diego Surf Dawgs. Over the years, the GBL tried to create waves by bringing in former Major League stars and Ronnie went out on a limb and recruited former home run champion Jose Canseco to play for the Surf Dawgs.

Sadly, the day after Canseco was signed, he requested a trade to the Long Beach team. As a form of "revenge" during a road trip, Ronnie purchased a whole load of juice boxes, printed Canseco's face and pasted it to the boxes to poke fun about the fact that Canseco had been using steroids (also known as "juicing up") during much of his career. The story gained instant national exposure, appearing on ESPN SportsCenter and giving the league some great publicity.

The Canseco incident proved to Ronnie that everyone loves a good story, no matter how prominent the product. Ronnie was also an avid fan of 2K's games and would frequently post on the game maker's forums. In 2008, the company was in need of forum managers for their games and recruited one of their biggest fans, Ronnie, to move back home to the Bay Area and join the company.

One thing that gets you about Ronnie is his ability to empathize because he is a member of the target group. On his ability to blend into the 2K Sports portfolio, Ronnie says, "I probably sit most as a sports fan. I played games but I wasn't super hard-core. Definitely my 'in' was sports."

One aspect that's important to remember is that no single person is 100% like the brand (unless you actually own the brand). So there's a kind of evolution of the individual that has to take place on one hand, but also an understanding that the product you sell is not exclusive to just that universe. For Ronnie, history had made his background unusually suitable for the gaming industry. "The cross between a jock and a gamer nerd has never been so blurry. I played sports in college and now it feels that there's such a competitive element to gaming that sports and gamers are more similar than ever before."

After serving as a forum manager for some time, the company realized the potential power of social media and asked Ronnie to head up their efforts. Interestingly, the company's decision to allow the Ronnie2K character to evolve was not necessarily solely due to marketing purposes. "We needed someone to speak freely and not worry about legal approvals," says Ronnie. "There's such an approval process for a corporate statement. Ronnie2K was invented to combat the whole issue of speaking without worrying about legal implications. It became such a popular thing that I've gained the trust of my company. I use my own judgment. My tweets are also pushing the brand and the newest game or initiative or trailer. The core of social media is to connect people to people. It is a scary proposition that legal teams have to have faith in and you have to be there long term if you want to be the face of the company."

But while Ronnie is now in his sixth year with the company, unexpectedly, it took more than four years before the persona really took off. Initially, the progression was gradual as Ronnie started with 8,000 Twitter followers and only reached about 20,000 by the summer of 2012. So while 2K's sales have grown 10 to 12-fold since Ronnie started with the company, it turns out that nearly 90% of his following appeared in the last 18 months.

Being in charge of digital media, Ronnie's job involves storytelling on a daily basis, something that would not be possible if he was in the PR field where editors have a lot of gaming information to process on a daily basis. So Ronnie does everything from making announcements and previews about upcoming launch dates and important features of the game, talking to celebrities about their game experience and really telling the story of how the game's simulations can appeal to certain innate human needs in the second decade of the 21st century such as personalization, newness and the idea of achieving personal experience.

Many of the game functions, such as creating your own team, playing on behalf of your favorite team or even creating yourself as a character in the game (and all the drama that goes along with it), relates to these trends. Ronnie's job is to find connectivity between these functions and the emotional triggers that they pull. In essence he "connects the dots" between the game's functions and the user's psychological social needs. Perhaps this is the greatest epitome of empathy.

Ronnie credits his personal relatability to the success of his story. "People can relate to me, they can connect better to a person as compared to a brand. I can speak more freely but am more relatable to the consumer. I'm a video game fan who happens to work for a video game company. I'm kind of 'living my dream' and that's a story a lot of people can relate to. There's a need for a story you can tell as a person that a company can't. Social media is a network of connectivity. You can't connect with a person as a brand as you can with a person. It's a lot easier to have a network of connectivity as a person."

We're Only Human

If we look at the NBA 2K12 or 2K13 games, which really created the buzz, we can see that Ronnie's position as an "insider" who would "leak" important upcoming information was a key element to this. First comes the announcement of the game, then the cover, the trailer and some insights into the new game features. This all leads up to the actual launch of the game which last year was done in Times Square. But really what draws people to the brand through that developing campaign is the daily storytelling of Ronnie.

Interestingly, Ronnie notes that part of the company's story isn't about the company at all. Certainly, while his ability to hobnob with the very idols of his customers and to share insights on those meetings is one critical element of the value of his story, it's often his ability to simply talk as a sports fan that brings him untold attention.

A case in point was during the 2013 Super Bowl. Shortly after a stunning halftime show highlighted by Beyoncé, the teams came out and on the opening play of the half, Jacoby Jones of the Baltimore Ravens ran the kickoff back for a touchdown. Ronnie promptly tweeted "I think Jacoby Jones was trying to catch Beyoncé before she left the building".[44] It was, as Ronnie puts it, "just being a male in his late-20s and most of my followers could relate to that". The end result? 7,000 re-tweets.

What we can see from the 2K Games experience is a major lesson on relatability and the power of tying a person to the brand. Ronnie makes a great point

---

44   Tweet by @Ronnie2K, February 3, 2013.

in saying that he is living "every sports gamer's dream". While social media like Twitter in particular has given the normal sports fan (or music fan), the ability to get a window on their favorite celebrity's everyday life, Ronnie instead uses social media to act as a kind of mix between "a source close to the company told me..." and "my friend, the sports fan". Ronnie is that inside window to the entire journey of the 2K product. People see the origins of the features, the development process and then get this incredibly relatable review of how awesome the new features really are from a figure they trust.

In fact, we are looking for heroes who are living in a world of fantasy. Think of it this way. If you worked for a retailer, technically you could try on and talk about every piece of clothing in the store. But for most people, they don't have the money to have the personal experience with more than just a couple of products, although they certainly would fantasize to do so. So invariably, people live vicariously through a personal maven like @Ronnie2K. If ever there was a way to distill the concept of the journey into one powerful test, the "living vicariously through this guy" test would absolutely be it.

Interestingly, we also learn that while the strategy seems perfectly clear to most, the biggest obstacle to adopting such transparency and commitment to opening up the journey is internal. While most companies embrace social media as a great tool, very few actually understand it. Invariably, they try to use social media as a kind of "miracle drug" to gaining empathy and achieving relatability to their customers and in doing so sanitize their story to the point that it becomes nothing more than a sales pitch. In Ronnie Singh's case, it was the trust of the Senior Vice President of Marketing of 2K Games that allowed him to split off from the corporate message and build the brand. But without a full organizational buy-in, that personality could never be entirely genuine nor the journey so vivid to Ronnie's followers.

A Further Note: Bringing it Back to Pre-Launch

Before leaving the story of Ronnie Singh, it's worth relating a few other lessons that come back to our pre-launch phase. First, notice that Ronnie's core similarity to the customer base and understanding of social trends directly enables him to not only understand his customers and empathize with them, but also to speak in their language. 2K made a terrific decision to hire from among their customers. He is a passionate gamer and as such had the capacity to quick sync his personal voice with that of the business.

Second, as part of empathizing with customers, personality-based marketing allows him to "re-humanize" the brand's discussion with its customers. By anticipating the kind of information they might want and also by speaking in a tone that is free and casual, his information is timely, semi-exclusive and more like a person talking to friends than an overt "buy my product message".

Finally, we learn that there is rarely a single individual who can seamlessly represent the brand from the onset. The process of effective relatable storytelling starts with the storytellers using their inherent connection to the brand and adding a few "missing links" to get them in perfect harmony with their audience. This may mean adjusting their tone to be more technical (depending on the consumer) or it may involve them matching their inherent interests with an underlying psychological foundation of the customers. Ronnie Singh manages to do that merely by tweaking his personality to be a better fit with the 2K brand.

So while all the psychology of the pre-launch phase may seem at first a bit overwhelming, it is worth noting how instrumental it was in Ronnie Singh and 2K ever finding each other in the first place and in contributing to the runaway success that relationship has been ever since. After all, a journey is nothing if there isn't a great storyteller to lead people *en route*.

EIGHT

SUPERSIZE ME

Using Real People to Take the Journey to the Next Level

GANDHI: If we obtain our freedom by murder and bloodshed I want no part of it.
NEHRU: It was one incident.
GANDHI: Tell that to the families of the policemen who died.
NEHRU: Bapu – the whole nation is marching. They wouldn't stop, even if we asked them to.
GANDHI: I will ask. And I will fast as penance for my part in arousing such emotions – and I will not stop until they stop.
NEHRU: But – but Gandhiji people are aroused . . . they won't stop.
GANDHI: If I die, perhaps they will . . .

- Gandhi (1982)[45]

---

45   Gandhi. Dir. Richard Attenborough. Columbia Pictures, 1982.

One of the major elements of any good story is to take a grand mission and drive it down to people to whom we can relate. We talked already about empathy and how in the modern age, people want to be able to connect to individuals. Subway used Jared Fogle, Nike used Michael Jordan and the Indian nation was inspired by Mahatma Gandhi.

We talked earlier about TOMS and Blake Mycoskie's journey. One thing that stands out about the story behind the brand is that it doesn't revolve around things and places, but rather about people. When Blake speaks, he talks about the women who brought him to his first village and the kids receiving their shoes. He talks about his polo teacher Alejo, who encouraged him to think bigger than just one village. He talks about his epiphany. In a sense, Blake becomes a protagonist in his own brand's story. His journey, his path to goodness, becomes the underlying story that would eventually lead TOMS from being merely a simple comfortable country shoe, to becoming a cause that does much more. Taken to an extreme, many of the most devoted TOMS buyers feel like they are taking on part of the journey with Blake.

In his book, Blake says, "When you have a memorable story about who you are and what your mission is, your success no longer depends on how experienced you are or how many degrees you have or who you know. A good story transcends boundaries, breaks borders and opens doors."[46]

But the stories don't stop there. One element of journey storytelling is how new epics are written all the time by real people. Blake likes to tell the story of a woman he spotted at an airport wearing TOMS shoes. He approached her incognito and asked her what she thought of the shoes. She proudly re-told Blake's life story to him (not entirely accurately, but hey, becoming a modern-day legend doesn't hurt the credibility of your company) in vivid detail and practically yelled at Blake about how he *had* to get a pair of TOMS shoes ... well, until he told her he was Blake.

What we learn about the story is that the journey and re-telling of key incidents through characters that form the mosaic of a story not only strengthens the brand's identity; it also creates a reason for existence that is so crystal clear that it demands to be followed.

---

46   From "Start Something That Matters" by Blake Mycoskie, Spiegel and Grau, 2011.

How a Bombing Led to a New Thunder in Oklahoma City

The idea of humanizing the story of a brand is not exclusive to the business world. Over the course of 2006 and 2007, intensive negotiations resulted in the sale of the Seattle Supersonics NBA team, one of the most historic franchises in the league, to a group of Oklahoma City-based investors led by Clay Bennett. Eighteen months later, having rejected multiple efforts by the City of Seattle to keep the Sonics, Bennett and his team relocated the Sonics to Oklahoma City and in 2008, the Thunder were born.

While the move of the Sonics is seen by many as a black eye on the term of NBA commissioner David Stern, with many in Seattle still believing that former Sonics owner Howard Schultz, Bennett and the NBA conspired to betray them, something quite remarkable has happened in Oklahoma City as the team has been fully embraced as an integral part of the local community.

Due to the relatively small size of the market the Thunder's ability to generate off-court revenue which makes up a considerable amount of a team's value is significantly more limited than say cities like New York or Los Angeles.[47] Nevertheless, during the ensuing four seasons, Bennett's team, led by General Manager Sam Presti, were successful in developing a team that would go on to the NBA Finals.

The big story though is not the success of the team but rather in their ability to keep their star players like scoring champ Kevin Durant and point guard Russell Westbrook. Knowing their limited revenue opportunities, Presti and his team have been so successful at weaving the community and the concept of the team together so tightly that players actually are taking a discount to play in a tiny city like OKC, far away from the bright lights of many other lucrative markets.

Why would they do that? Well, one interesting element of the Thunder's indoctrination process is to bring prospective players immediately to the very essence of why the team is vital to the Oklahoma City community.

The story starts in 1992. For years, Timothy McVeigh, a Gulf War veteran and anti-government activist, gradually developed an active hatred in all things government, from its imposition of taxes to the handling of the cult crisis at Waco, Texas, in 1993. McVeigh came up with a plan to detonate a bomb that would strike at

---

47 Oklahoma City ranks something like the 45th largest TV market in the US, which is pretty unusual when there are just 30 NBA teams.

the very institution he hated most, the US government. Along with co-conspirator Terry Nichols, they prepared a Ryder moving truck filled with nearly 5,000 pounds of explosives, parked it in a drop-off zone in front of the Alfred P. Murrah Federal Building and lit a 5-minute fuse. At 9:02, the fuse detonated and blew out the entire north face of the building killing 168 people inside.

The disaster left deep scars on this close-knit community. In a small town, most people "know someone who knows someone". And in truth, a small town like Oklahoma City rarely possesses anything like a sports team that can serve as a rallying point for civic pride.[48]

When the Thunder came to town, Presti was sure to incorporate the Oklahoma City bombings story into what made the team so important. It's said that every new player is required to visit the memorial for the victims, in order to see first-hand why it is so important for them to make a long-term commitment to the community. It's not that players are intrinsically unselfish and don't look for money, but part of the whole concept of "team" for the Thunder has been founded based on the story of the bombings and the team members not just being basketball players but an essential part of the Oklahoma City community. To many of them, the opportunity to play in OKC is a privilege. So a lot of players eventually stay on.

There's no question that the Oklahoma City Thunder are a great and entertaining basketball team. The opportunity to watch Kevin Durant, one of the sweetest shooting players ever to play the game, or Russell Westbrook, certainly one of the most exciting, 41 times a year is incentive enough for people to get out and support the team. But in the end, the Thunder's journey starts two decades ago and everyone is aware of it, either directly through incoming players visiting the site for the first time or intrinsically for the people of the community who have in some way experienced the impact, either psychologically or perhaps in the actual loss of a loved one. The story internally is so strong that it weaves its way into the fabric of the team's reason for being.

As a New Yorker or San Franciscan, you might still like the Thunder for their great players. But for the 18,203 people who pack the Chesapeake Energy Arena 41 times (plus a few playoff games) a year, the Thunder are a way of bringing together a community that is searching for something positive that they can always hold onto.

---

48 To see how important a sports team can be to a devastated area, one need look no further than the incredibly emotional return of the New Orleans Saints to the Superdome on September 25, 2006, after Hurricane Katrina or the emotional speech of David Ortiz to fans on the day the Boston Red Sox returned to Fenway Park in the aftermath of the April 2013 Boston Marathon bombings.

The Ultimate Journey

To them, the Thunder are more than a basketball team, they are a civic institution. To the Thunder players, the Oklahoma City fans are more than fans, they are their community.

Just as a final note, if you follow the Thunder players, you see a lot of photos of them visiting hospitals, greeting fans and hosting parties for disadvantaged children. Each of these stories represents an awesome event and feeds into the continuing cycle of the Thunder journey.

A Personal Story

I always like to re-tell a specific story to partners, friends and pretty much anyone I meet about how we demonstrated that we would be a "people first" company truly dedicated to "Making Special People Look and Feel Amazing".

In early 2010, we were just beginning our journey to figuring out why the watches and handbags we sold in our division were more than just items that people put on their wrist or over their shoulder but rather were an essential part of a person's own personal happiness and sense of self-identity. In a sea of discounts, we were having trouble actually demonstrating to people that we weren't "all about the money" like everyone else.

I was attending a training session by the Disney Institute, when a call came across about a customer who was in a tremendous quandary. Aside from selling through our own retail stores, we distributed watches to independent "Ma and Pa" watch shops. Apparently, a customer had purchased a watch from one of these authorized shops and paid full price. A couple of months later, the watch broke and he brought it to our service center to be fixed. When the technicians opened the watch, they discovered the watch was a fake.

I first went to our Service Centre head and asked, "So what should we do?" He explained to me that since we didn't sell the watch and it wasn't our fault, we shouldn't take on any responsibility but maybe we could give a voucher so the customer would feel better.

I then asked our sales manager the same question and he suggested we arrange a meeting between the customer and the owner of the store and facilitate him in getting his money back or finding a win-win solution.

Not being an expert, I would generally defer to whichever of the two opinions seemed better. But I was troubled. On the one hand, we were basically denying any responsibility and giving a concession prize (a voucher) just to kind of "get rid" of the customer. On the other, the sales guys were willing to let the dealer act in such a callous manner and face no penalties other than maybe returning some money and causing the customer to walk into what would clearly be a high-stress confrontation.

So after talking within our team, we decided to do something that sent a message. We told both departments that we rejected their ideas. Instead, first, we would cut the dealer effective immediately. That dealership's actions were downright unethical, irrespective of how much business we did with them a year. It was our responsibility to protect customers from such people. Second, we instructed the team to contact the customer and ask him to come to any of our stores anytime and pick out an original product of his choice. Third, we made sure this decision was informed to the entire team. At the time I recall saying to the team, "This is our moment to shine.

I followed up with the customer about a week later and he was incredibly grateful for the decision that we had taken, even without him asking. He let us know that he would tell all of his friends about how we solved his problem.

From then on, the entire mood of the department changed and our team members started finding the best solution for their customers without even asking for approval. And why not? It's when the choices are really hard that you demonstrate who you really are.

In the last three years, I've told this story at least a hundred times and you can see the expressions of amazement on people's faces whenever they hear it. You see, after all "Making Special People Look and Feel Amazing" hasn't been a job, it's been a developing epic.

Again, the reason for relaying this story is not to give you a mundane look at the innards of our business. Furthermore, not every case ends as well as this one and in fact we are still working to be better at making everyone happy.

The key point is that this particular case has become a story that we share with everyone, new recruits, mall owners, brands and people we just meet. By invoking our characters and making it about humans instead of something faceless and corporate, the story has so much more resonance. In many ways, it becomes a defining symbol of who we are and what we stand for. Stories like this have become a part of our brand's journey, no different than Blake Mycoskie writing or speaking about his trip to Argentina or Dave Nichol chasing that elusive perfect cookie. [49]

49 While I re-tell our story under Blake's, there is no question that what he and the TOMS organization achieved is truly world-changing to a degree to which we could only aspire. For more information, I absolutely recommend you read his book or visit TOMS.com.

Finishing the Alley-Oop

Not every brand has such a direct human interaction like Blake's shoe drive or Sam Presti's guided tour of a bomb site but even for those of us who have corporate missions that are moderately-sized but well intentioned nevertheless, there is a role in humanizing our interactions as a way of telling our ongoing story and journey.

In creating a running human narrative for your story, there are a few things to always remember.

Lesson 1 – Transparency

Do bare your soul for all to see. You can't simply say "there was a problem so we solved it." Rather, you have to go through the logical steps of the process, never leaving out the trials and tribulations you or your company experienced to get to your current point.

Lesson 2 - The Timing Aspect

Great stories rarely happen in an instant without some contributing factor. Never forget to start at the true beginning and don't "skip chapters".

Lesson 3 - The Human Element

It cannot be said enough that your story MUST contain people. Whether it's the founder, your employee who travelled the world to find the product, or a customer or acquaintance who inspired your company's product or mission, those are what will make the journey really pop and are the difference between a dry, factual account of an event and a truly epic, legendary call to action.[50]

In the past, brands often avoided sharing their journey and the characters who had been or are a part of it. Perhaps this omission is due to some fear that others might take the same road and ultimately become competitors, perhaps because they didn't want the characters to become bigger than the brand. The journey simply cannot be told without including the human element. This is what puts soul in your brand.

---

50 One of my favorite books of all time is "A Fortune Teller Told Me" by Tiziano Terzani, a fascinating account of a long trip he took through Southeast Asia and the various people he met along the way. The stories practically come to life before you. Good writing and storytelling in business are pretty much the same thing.

Think back to the earlier chapter on empathy. The journey of a great brand, just like our own lives, is an ongoing saga. Having real people is what fuels the incredible power of empathy in your story, thereby inspiring present and future customers and partners. If you can master the art of humanizing your journey, even a small brand in size can be a huge brand in stature.

To close this section, it's important to revisit the fundamentals of what we've learned about storytelling using the concept of journey storytelling. There are four key steps to the concept, those being the Idea, the Process, the End Product and the Awesome Event. The fundamental idea here is that your ability as a storyteller to leap past the outdated approach of keeping everything silent and instead inviting the world to know your brand and product better will make you not merely accepted but potentially loved. Journeys represent a way for you to establish relevance in the lives of your customers creating a community instead of a market. If you are able to instill passion and establish a connection to what people have always been thinking or hoping for, you can create something that is uniquely powerful.

Once you have mastered the idea of the Journey and are starting to think about what pieces might work in your story, it's time to fine-tune the actual end product with some useful techniques. It's time to lift off.

LIFT OFF:
MORE TECHNIQUES FOR STRUCTURING, CHECKING AND EVALUATING YOUR STORY

NINE

I THINK I SORTA' KINDA' MUST LOVE YA

Using "So What?" to Find The REAL Story

TIM: Follow only if ye be men of valor, for the entrance to this cave is guarded by a creature so foul, so cruel that no man yet has fought with it and lived! Bones of a full fifty men lie strewn about its lair. So, brave knights, if you do doubt your courage or your strength, come no further, for death awaits you all with nasty, big, pointy teeth.
ARTHUR: Where?
TIM: There!
ARTHUR: What, behind the rabbit?
TIM: It is the rabbit!
ARTHUR: You silly sod!
TIM: What?
ARTHUR: You got us all worked up!
TIM: Well, that's no ordinary rabbit.

- Monty Python and the Holy Grail (1975)[51]

---

51 Monty Python and the Holy Grail. Dir. Terry Gilliam, Terry Jones. EMI Films, 1975.

It's hard to imagine that a simple bunny rabbit could wipe out a whole platoon of brave knights, right? The previous scene is a good example of the importance of being a reliable and believable storyteller. When it comes to telling a story about your products, trust is everything. Now in "The Holy Grail", nobody believes the story of the ferocious rabbit … that is, until a knight approaches it and has his head bitten off in one fell swoop by the killer bunny.

Many marketers feel that just by having a brand, customers will take a shot at "approaching the rabbit", whereas in very few cases do they even know where to find the bunny (a.k.a. the brand) in the first place. The classical way of building a story is to simply take the most "marketable" features and functions of our products, put some fluffy words around them and create a press release. But as I mentioned at the end of the previous chapter, that's really just a case of falling into the trap of the "98% Rule". We want to move away from that.

So how can we do that? Perhaps that's the wrong question. The better question is actually "So What?" When we ask "So What?" we can tie together empathy and passion to make the foundations of a great story. This also allows you to figure out whether the foundation of your story is sufficiently compelling to make a dent in the clutter of voices that customers hear on a daily basis.

I'm Not Good Enough, But "So What?"

When I was younger, I always had a bit of a confidence deficit, meaning that I viewed myself as a "peripheral" part of the lives of many of the people I knew as opposed to being the "lead actor". It's kind of like playing sports in school and being the last person chosen for the team. You would like to scream and shout that you're good enough, but nobody can hear you.

Actually, all of us have this sense of insecurity in different ways. Some of us mask it better than others. I've had so many friends (especially teens and twenty-somethings) who ask themselves, "What if there's nobody out there for me?" or "What if I don't turn out as well as my parents?" Insecurity is a normal psychological expression for humans arising from some idealized way of seeing those around us – essentially, seeing the world in a "the grass is always greener" way.

In most cases, insecurity is viewed as a bad thing, albeit very human. Insecurity prevents us from starting a new business, quitting a job we hate, telling people what we think, approaching the girl/boy we really like, etc.

However, when it comes to storytelling, insecurity is actually empowering because it forces us to re-think all of our assumptions about our product and brand and come up with a *raison d'être* that is actually more compelling than if we just assumed "We're great!" Once we realize that people won't automatically look for our product or brand, we have to start thinking of the justifications for why we should be more than just an "extra" in the "film of life" of our friends, guests and customers. "So What?" helps us to do that.

I've been using the "So What?" method for many years without knowing where it originated. Then, shortly after I started writing this book, I discovered there's a variation of this theory called the "Five Levels of Why", which is an integral part of Six Sigma methodology in identifying the root of any given problem[52]

Here's an example:

You are working in a financial planning firm. Every day, you pore over mounds of paper to help people figure out where to invest their money or how to file their taxes. So what are you really doing?

The Impassionate View

"I help people file their taxes so their life is easier and I help them plan their finances so they can make and keep more money."

I would guess close to 99% of the world sees the entire financial planning industry in that way. For most people, financial planning is as about as exciting as watching paint dry. But if you wanted to get passionate about financial planning and to tell a story about it, you would go a bit deeper.

Level 1:

"As a financial planner, I help people file their taxes and plan their finances."
"So What?"

Level 2:

"By helping them with their taxes, people can save a lot of money and if I help them plan, they can keep a lot more money and enjoy more things."
"So What?"

---

52   If you want to find out more about Six Sigma, you can check out isixsigma.com or read any of the many books on how John F. Mitchell and his team at Motorola initially came around to this idea.

Level 3:

"Umm. People get upset about paying a lot of taxes. Think of all the things they can buy and how much more comfortable they would be if they paid less tax."

"SO WHAT?"

Level 4:

"Getting people to save money on their taxes and better plan their finances is about quality of life and about achieving dreams. Money is a way for people to achieve their ambitions in life, whether it's to do great things or merely to find security for their family."

"Ok getting there, SO WHAT!?!"

Level 5:

"If people can achieve their dreams, their lives become purposeful. We only have a short time on this planet and we want to live life to the fullest. If we find ways to save our clients' money, we are adding to the quality of their life. Think of all those great memories they could have when they go on a trip with their loved ones or buy a new toy to make their child smile. Think about how that money could be enough to buy tuition or entry to the best college so a parent could say they gave their child a chance at the greatest future possible."

"And think of the amazing things that a person can do with those extra funds later in life. Instead of barely surviving and waiting for their days to end (or having them end faster if they can't afford proper health care), we can allow them to travel, to go back to school, to do activities that they've always dreamed of but never had time to do or even, heaven forbid, afford a medical technology and level of care that they might never have if they didn't have the funds to afford it."

"In short ... our job is about guiding them to a better future."

Getting to Level 5

Level 5 is a lot more compelling than Level 1, isn't it?

That Level 5 description is the essence of a family planning business. Most financial planners will never achieve or articulate that level of self-awareness of their business and thus become entirely commoditized. But I can assure you that any good planner who communicates that explanation in Level 5 is never going to have a problem getting business.

Now there's a lot more to this story than just passion. We see in this simple explanation context and purpose. But above all, if you were able to ask yourself "So What?" enough times, you would think that you would be a lot more excited and enthusiastic to tell the story, right?

In doing the "So What?" exercise and putting yourself in the shoes of even the most cynical (but not impossible) customer, you might just notice that you are starting to tell the story in *their* terms, not the classic marketing template that others you know learned in school and which never progressed from there.

A to Z in 4.5 seconds

So how many "So Whats?" does it take before you get to the crux of your story? Well, there's no set answer for that. It really depends on how inspired you start out.

Beginners will probably take four to five steps to get to something that excites them while the best writers tend to intrinsically get to the right answer in a maximum of two steps. If you see a great writer or storyteller who "just gets it", it is usually because they have trained their brain to get right to the end of the process while skipping all the intermediate steps.

I need to emphasize here that the "So What?" method is *not* about finding gimmicks to get people to buy your product but rather quite the opposite. Gimmicks and marketing tricks are what you use when you don't know your brand or product's true utility to its customers. "So What?" provides you with a unique insight that allows you to speak to the heart of your guest. It is the foundation of what you should communicate. From that starting point, you can build a style guide that defines all of your communication tools (including press releases, marketing materials and even how you answer the phones at your office).

In the case of the financial planner I mentioned, your story and writing would not focus on your rates or saving money. Rather, all of your communication would focus on what past clients were able to do with the money they saved (e.g.: "put my first kid through college", "took the vacation I always dreamed of"). Perhaps you might write a manifesto (we'll discuss this later). This can even be adopted to your process of doing business where your first appointment (often called your "Financial Check-Up" – ugh! Who likes to go for a check-up?) could even have an uplifting name like say, the "Dream Assessment".

If you want to sharpen your "So What?" skills, practice is the best way. You can use even the most mundane, unremarkable objects that you see in your daily life and start coming up with story ideas: your day at school, your child's conversation, your lunch, or anything else you want. Practicing this is a bit like training for the Olympics; the more you do it, the higher you can jump or faster you can run.

Later on, I'll tell the story of my friend Edward Suhadi, who runs a photo and video production company. He has expertly used the "So What?" rule to promote to his clients that people don't hire wedding photographers to simply take pre-choreographed moments, but to make the wedding into a true "storybook" by re-interpreting how spontaneous events happened. His pitch had made taking your standard wedding photos into something more like "Starring in the World's Happiest Love Novel".

The "So What?" Method is a powerful way to align your thinking process whenever you start writing or telling a story. It helps you to evaluate whether your journey is not only relevant but also compelling to your target customer from both a functional and an emotional perspective. It helps you separate which part of the journey is worth telling and which is worth skipping. It also allows you to compress your journey into a length that is easy to grasp and remember.

By hammering down the "So What?", you can start to define a tone for your brand's storytelling. That's what we'll discuss next.

TEN

I'M THAT GUY, AND THAT GUY IS ME

The Power of Relatability and Tone

VIZZINI: I can't compete with you physically, and you're no match for my brains.
MAN IN BLACK: You're that smart?
VIZZINI: Let me put it this way: Have you ever heard or Plato, Aristotle, Socrates?
MAN IN BLACK: Yes.
VIZZINI: Morons!

- The Princess Bride (1987)[53]

53   The Princess Bride. Dir. Rob Reiner. 20th Century Fox, 1987.

In "The Princess Bride", this confrontation between a daring swashbuckler (the man in black) trying to rescue a princess from Vizzini, a seemingly cerebral kidnapper and his gang, illustrates the importance of tone. If you watch the entire scene, the man in black then challenges Vizzini to a kind of shell game, placing a deadly poison into two glasses. Vizzini tries to get the man in black to tip his hand by using his "superior intellect". In the end, it turns out that the game was actually rigged by the man in black and Vizzini dies not by the sword, but by the poisoned chalice. It seems that the man in black has both brains and brawn while it turns out that Vizzini has neither.

Vizzini's fatal flaw is his arrogance. If we look at the way he talks, he does everything in his power to not only outwit his adversary but also offer the tone of a deeply intelligent, rational person. By getting it wrong, he gives the man in black a deeper understanding that Vizzini is, in fact, a buffoon.

This is what happens when you get your storytelling tone wrong.

The easiest way to avoid this trap is to use characters to set a tone for your journey. We talked earlier about empathy. Now let's add in the concept of tone. Tone is your ability to adapt your personal "Inner Voice" and match it to how your customers would expect you to talk if your brand was a real person, someone to whom they can relate.

Think of it this way:

Empathy + Tone = Relatability

Fans of the TV series "House" will remember Hugh Laurie as the rambunctious New England doctor who uses bitter sarcasm and logical thought to diagnose unexplainable diseases in his patients. Fewer people know that Laurie is actually British. According to most descriptions of Laurie, he is a "moody Brit". So actually his Inner Voice had the moody part down but without the American accent, he would have been less believable as Dr. Gregory House. Tone mattered and it eventually won him two Golden Globe Awards.

Tone is related to emotions. Emotions are something that makes us human and allows others to empathize with us. As F. Scott Fitzgerald once wrote:

"You've got to sell your heart, your strongest reactions, not the little minor things that only touch you lightly, the little experiences that you might tell at dinner. This is especially true when you begin to write, when you have not yet developed the tricks of interesting people on paper, when you have none of the technique which it takes time to learn. When, in short, you have only your emotions to sell."

Fitzgerald really hits the nail on the head. When you write or present, you need to really "leave it all out there" for people to feel your emotions.

While many people do respect a humble storyteller who has gone from rags to riches, keeping a humble tone isn't necessarily the only way to go. You can look at different voices of CEOs and influential celebrities and note that their respective tones can be quite different. Sir Richard Branson is viewed by many as a bit cheeky (to use a very British word), Steve Jobs was impassioned, Michael Kors can be brutally honest while Mark Zuckerberg is viewed by some as evasive yet visionary. Karl Lagerfeld of Chanel may not be warm and fuzzy but he is iconic with a defined style and taste, perfect for the Chanel customer who wants to be seen as standing above the crowd. In the end, there is no one single right tone that makes every company relatable. Every brand needs to have its own individual personality and tone.

Humble Pie

That said, while high-fliers or corporate bodies tend to get a free pass to speak in any of a number of tones, when it comes down to ordinary people, honesty and modesty are often worth their weight in gold.

In early-2012, my wife and I took a three-week backpacking trip to Vietnam. As with backpacking anywhere, these trips are not so much about the places you go as much as the people you meet.

During the most difficult leg of our trip, a 13-hour train ride between the central town of Hue to the capital of Hanoi, we found ourselves in a four-person cabin with an Irish couple based in Australia. Obviously, over the course of 13 hours, you can get to know people pretty well. The people we were with had a story that was one of the most inspirational you could imagine.

Steve and Ashley are seasoned travellers. Ashley was a marketing consultant while Steve had carved out a nice career as a civil engineer specializing in development projects. As my wife was pregnant at the time, the conversation eventually came around to the "So, do you have kids?" question. Ashley replied that they didn't but for a reason.

It turns out that this trip was a bit of a celebration. The couple was celebrating the five-year anniversary of Steve being declared cured of cancer. In the meantime, Ashley admitted that she had her own problems earlier in life including being institutionalized for clinical depression.

So while the couple had not had kids, they spent their lives doing what they loved, traveling and helping people. Each year, they spent a minimum of two weeks volunteering on development projects and about four to six months just traveling around and experiencing the world. Steve was talking about starting a business as a trainer.

If you want to talk about likability and relatability and empathy, just try talking to people who have been through what Steve and Ashley had experienced in their lives. When a person can overcome that kind of adversity, others will automatically stop and listen. Not only can we empathize with their circumstances, they present an authoritative figure you would never think to question. In fact, if anything, you want to hear more.

People like Steve and Ashley tend not to boast about their "victory" and in fact, if you hear them speak, it's rather the opposite. They are actually quite introspective and even "shy" to talk about it. At the same time, there's a quiet confidence that they tend to project their desire to teach others about the ability of the human soul to overcome adversity. This creates an instant ability for others to relate to them. That shyness is their "tone". You could imagine if Steve spent all his time boasting about how he beat cancer, you might not root for him quite as hard. It's that tint of modesty that means everything.

Imagine a brand talking about a journey that started from the founders overcoming personal adversity, like Steve and Ashley had, as part of their journey to create a product. A humble tone that enhances empathy can help create a story to which people can do more than relate; they can fall in love with it.

A Place Called Hope

Even in cases where your company doesn't have a story of personal adversity, sometimes a human face can tip the empathy side of the equation.

Think about Subway's famous "Jared" commercials in which the company promised you could lose gobs of weight by eating Subway sandwiches (and eating in moderate amounts with ample exercise). Had the Subway marketing people simply said "Eat Subway Sandwiches, Lose Lots of Weight!" that might not have been particularly impactful. Of course, Subway does not inherently possess a story of overcoming adversity like Steve and Ashley. By all accounts, it's not a company to which anyone can relate. However, by exposing the narrative of Jared Fogle's struggle to change his life and how the company's product helped him to get there, Subway gained both empathy and an entirely different tone as a champion of healthy eating. People related to Jared and thus could relate to Subway in a more emotional way.

Yet make no mistake, this was not a marketing ploy that could have been dreamed up. Jared was not an "invention" of a marketing agency. He had taken it upon himself to lose weight simply because a Subway outlet was close to his college dorm and his story was brought to a Chicago franchisee who related it to the company.

As the story goes, even company officials didn't originally want to use Jared given they were afraid of being held liable by people who didn't end up losing weight. Subway executives faced a dilemma not much different than 2K Games faced when they allowed Ronnie Singh to become the "face of the franchise". In the end, they rightly realized that changing the tone of the company was a risk worth taking.

Jared was a normal guy who consumed about 700 sandwiches in a year and lost 245 pounds. This guy truly had been through adversity. Who wouldn't want to take inspiration from that? More importantly, who wouldn't want to eat a sandwich from a company that helped him achieve this incredible feat?

Tone for Corporate Entities

The angle of an individual's story of courage is not always possible to achieve. Consider how many in the luxury industry parade out their CEOs, people who we admire as designers perhaps but who do not have an inspiring story of overcoming adversity *per se*. There are a lot of companies out there for whom neither the CEO nor any other company official ever appears and is hardly known except by a few who really know the industry. For example, could you name the CEO of H&M? How about Caterpillar? Wal-Mart? Nestle?

In some cases, trotting out the wrong people (or having them exposed unintentionally) can actually harpoon your entire journey. A CEO who is seen as aloof and unconnected may actually create resentment from customers irrespective of the historical story of the brand.[54] Or think of a celebrity who is disliked by the public or may be boastful where the brand should be more humble.[55]

---

54 Financial industry CEOs almost all seem to fall into this category.

55 I've heard the term "Lindsay Lohan Syndrome" bandied around for just such a phenomena.

However, as people expect brands to be more and more like people, tone really matters more and more. Tone comes across in two ways. First, it's in the words you use. Second, it's in the way you use them.

Figuring Out the Right Tone

To write properly, you need to figure out your brand's tone, effectively the character you are being asked to play. So let's re-visit a diagram we used earlier and make a few changes with some examples:

MAP YOUR BRAND'S TONE

HUMOR

Serious — Outlandish

FORMALITY

Informal — Formal

BIGGEST STRENGTH

Functional — Emotional

VOLUME OF SPEECH

Quiet / Purposeful — Loud / Boastful

TRANSPARENCY

Ambiguity — Honesty

That gets you to health-check where you are at this point but if you want to get your language to a more relatable level, there are a few techniques that you can use.

Tip #1: The Us vs. You Debate

Most magazines in the market, particularly fashion or technology publications, give you the sense that they are shouting through a loudspeaker when they promote something. The reason is their use of either a neutral or third person tense when writing. If you write in the third person (i.e.: he, she, they or it) it's really as if you're trying to sell something, a truly difficult task in a world where the opinion of friends and family means so much and where everyone is a reviewer.

In fact, this is one reason why the whole blogging industry has grown in leaps and bounds over the years. Bloggers speak on personal opinion. It could well be that they are receiving some kind of financial reward from the brands that they are pitching but that is offset by the fact that they have built up credibility over time for speaking as themselves. The same goes for really good reviews on sites like Amazon, Agoda and Yelp!. In fact, the first person tone is so powerful that an entire industry of fake book review services grew up around Amazon to capitalize on people's willingness to trust the opinions of others based on how compelling were their written comments

To give an example:

Third-Person: The new iPhone is a great machine, full of exciting functions.

First-Person: We think the new iPhone is the best phone ever made by the company because of the incredible number of exciting new functions.

Notice the difference? In the third-person, the review is flat and seems contrived. In the first-person, not only does the first part of the review come off as being stronger because it's being "owned" by the reviewer, but even how we describe the rationale is stronger ("incredible number" vs. "full of"). Simply put, when we put ourselves into our story, we tend to be more emotional and usually our language comes off that way as well.

Tip #2: Make People Nod their Heads:

A lot of people think that pushing a product is all about explaining the whole range of functions. In the end, they come up with catchall phrases like "must-have" or "unbeatable". Actually, once you become a "must-have", you've already lost the storytelling game. Remember what we discussed earlier. People don't buy because you tell them they *have* to. Rather, they buy because your story is so compellingly tied to the emotions and aspirations in their lives that they *can't stop themselves* from making a purchase. I'll talk about Edward Suhadi in Chapter 15 but his idea that it's as if people are "nodding their heads" as you tell the story while thinking "Yes! I totally agree with that!" which is a truly appropriate image.

Most products in the world have lots of features and functions. But in truth, a unique blend of herbs and spices, a larger lithium battery or a fuel-injected engine with so many cc's of horsepower might seem compelling to marketers to talk about. In the end, none of these matter if they don't appeal to the lives of people who might use them.

Visually, the easiest way to communicate relatable specifics is by putting a character or a product in a position that evokes happy memories for them. People can visualize a chocolate chip cookie in which the packaging image consists of an endless facade of rich chocolate chips. People can visually associate lounging around on a Sunday afternoon reading a magazine on their iPad.

If you write, it's a bit different since you have to actually connect the dots for people.

Here's how most people do it:

Function/Feature 1 -> Function/Feature 2 -> Claim

"The new Blackberry Z10 has x number of GB of memory with an adaptable card and the function of Blackberry Cash which makes payment so much easier."

Pretty dull, right? Perhaps this is why Blackberry was (at time of writing) facing an uncertain future.

A better format is something like this:

Function/Feature -> Memory/Application + Negative Memory

"The new MacBook Air has this incredible new battery that lasts 10 hours so that you can bring your notebook around for an entire day without needing to recharge."

Notice how we tied the function up. We've been able to graduate from a generic, technical function to one that emphasizes applicability to how you think of the product.

Now here's a better one:

Positive Image -> Function/Application -> Application

"If you've never been to New York, it's one of the most fascinating cities on the planet. Just think of seeing rows of yellow taxi cabs, the Statue of Liberty, Broadway shows and

the hustle and bustle of people in Times Square and Wall Street. Singapore Airlines is now offering a non-stop Sydney to New York flight that arrives in 18 hours, saving you more than three hours. Anyone who's ever been on a long flight can tell you that every hour you save counts, now you can use the extra time to explore this magnificent city at your leisure."[56]

Tip #3: If Your Brand Isn't Relatable, Find Someone Who Is

There's one other even better step to the "nod their head" process.

Personal Experience -> Function/Application

"I remember during my last trip to New York, I used AirBnB to find an apartment and it was incredible. Their platform was so easy and the description and comments about the place we stayed at were right on the money."

Personal experience refers to the idea of using a spokesperson or endorser. But there's a catch. In the past, you could cart out "Celebrity X" and consumers would unquestionably believe everything the celebrity was saying. In the 21st century, things aren't so simple. If you want to talk about personal experience, it has to come from someone who has credibility, rather than just a simple mouthpiece.[57]

Think of ads for movies. It's long been a standard for film companies to take quotes from reviewers to make their film more marketable. If you've ever seen reviews like "The best drama of the year", "An Oscar-worthy performance" or "I was glued to my seat", you have to question whether people really believe in what's being written. It's no wonder they are more likely to check what people are saying on Twitter as opposed to the movie ads to form their preconceptions of a film.

Invariably, there are two ways for personal experience to be used more effectively:

1) Pick a person who has a history of "telling it how it is". People are deeply skeptical of guns for hire. Part of the appeal of the bloggers is that they don't give a "stamp of approval" for everything.

2) In the same breath as your endorser is espousing how great the product is, ensure that they also acknowledge that not everything is perfect. In the modern

---

56 Sadly, the direct Singapore to New York route, the world's longest flight, was recently cancelled. It's a shame too as many people I know who used that route raved about the time saved and convenience.

57 That said, in certain specific cases, you could simply cart out someone like Oprah Winfrey and the power of their community and their credibility by itself would be enough to sell your product.

world, imperfection is viewed not as an evil thing but as a sign of your brand and product's humanity. Nobody is perfect and people expect the same out of their products. The key thing is that the benefits of the product should far outweigh those imperfections.

There's no question that when you craft your message, it's one thing to be able to put together a good message, but when you and your people don't believe it and put it across in an arrogant or stiff manner, most people won't want to hear it. Herein lies the intersection between empathy and passion. You can't have success with one or the other; both need to be present in abundant quantity.

If you can get your tone right, it will give your journey and your storytelling in general authenticity. If customers perceive your brand as being fundamentally good and in line with their own values, they will buy. If your tone doesn't match your journey, they'll raise their guards. They'll go beyond not buying, they'll tell others why they're avoiding your products.

ELEVEN

LITTLE RED RIDING HOOD IN THE 21ST CENTURY

Structuring the Order of Your Story

CLAIRE: What would your friends say if we were walking down the hall to-gether? They'd laugh their asses off and you'd probably tell them you were doing it with me so they'd forgive you for being seen with me.
BENDER: Don't you ever talk about my friends! You don't know any of my friends, you don't look at any of my friends and you certainly wouldn't condescend to speak to any of my friends so you just stick to the things you know, shopping, nail polish, your father's BMW and your poor--rich--drunk mother in the Caribbean!
CLAIRE: Shut up!
BENDER: And as far as being concerned about what's gonna happen when you and I walk down the hallways at school, you can forget it! 'Cause it's never gonna happen! Just bury your head in the sand ... and wait for your fuckin' prom!

- The Breakfast Club (1985)[58]

---

58   The Breakfast Club. Dir. John Hughes. Universal Pictures, 1985.

When I was learning creative writing for the first time in school, the thought of writing a 250-word essay scared the daylights out of me. For many, the list of biggest life fears goes something like: public speaking, death and writing a 500-word essay (in that order). As my favorite saying goes, "the mountain always looks highest from the bottom." When you are writing your first word, those other 499 feel like scaling the heights of Everest itself. The 499th word is actually pretty easy as it turns out.

The biggest lesson I learned in my creative writing classes was the secret of fictional story construction. The basic levels of creative storytelling go something like this:

1) **The Introduction:** the initial stages of the story and the beginning of building the characters that would lead the story, in particular the hero (the protagonist) and maybe even the enemy (the antagonist).
2) **The Triggering Event:** that one action or event which, as Apple says, "changes everything". It's here that you can really make sense of the hero versus the villain.
3) **The Rising Action:** the plot begins to thicken as the series of events starts to unroll. Tensions build, relationships grow or start to break apart, the preface to battles are waged.
4) **The Climax**: the ultimate confrontation, that point in the story after which all the conflicts originating from the Triggering Event are basically resolved.
5) **The Falling Action**: the so-called happy ending as good returns to the world and all the tension from throughout the story dissipates
6) **The Denouement:** The surprise twist at the end where all hell breaks loose and where some new fact or turn of events is introduced which turns everything on its head (and usually leads to a sequel).

Notice that there's a logical flow to stories like this which are generally fictional in their approach and generally play out over the course of 200 or 300 pages, 120 minutes (the film adaptation) or 13 weeks times however many seasons (the made-for-TV version).

Fact is that all of our favorite dramas or sitcoms are founded in some way or another on this basic premise. Even stories we tell to our children are told the same way. For example, Little Red Riding Hood has a sick grandma, she sets out with steaming containers of chicken soup, comes across a wily wolf, the wolf races to grandma's house, eats her and dresses up like a woman (he must have been really hungry), attacks Little Red Riding Hood, she gets help from a passing woodcutter who proceeds to chop the wolf into pieces and everyone lives happily ever after.

The Ultimate Journey

Even our life stories generally follow classic storytelling construction – our childhood and schooling, a life-changing event, striving to achieve our goals, we succeed or fail, we resolve ourselves to the results and life goes on. Sometimes we have our own personal denouement where we either snatch victory from the jaws of defeat or vice versa. Probably we go through several classic storytelling constructions over the course of our lives.

In the business world, or even in a simple presentation, we generally don't have a chance at a sequel, let alone 300 pages. So how do we build a story structure that captures everything in a page?

Well, a bit of restructuring is necessary in such a case. I talked a bit about restructuring a product description in the last chapter through relatable specifics. This is great for selling pitches. Now let's take it a step further and talk about how you adapt your entire corporate story or large product launch story with a whole new structure.

Take the story of Little Red Riding Hood and see how we could re-write it if we were talking to a business audience. Inexperienced writers will follow classic storytelling structure and give you just the facts. It might go something like this.

We're happy to tell you about the story of Little Red Riding Hood. She's a wonderful little girl who bravely fended off a wily wolf that threatened to eat her. The wolf had stalked her through the woods for some time before getting to her grandma's house and eating her grandma. Eventually, Little Red Riding Hood discovered to her horror this wolf in her grandma's place and ran for her life before coming across a woodcutter. The brave woodcutter confronted and defeated the wolf, then chopped him into 2,000 pieces. Everyone lived happily ever after and enjoyed treats.
        -The end-

Interestingly, this is the way most people I know write press releases. Take a hypothetical example:

Samsung has this incredible tool that can let you do many things. We created the Note so that you can read stuff on it, draw on it and look very cool using it. Once you buy it, you will be instantly happy and use it a lot."
        -The end-

Or perhaps it could be a review for the next great party:

Playing this weekend at your favorite club is the world's #1 DJ, David Guetta. He started playing at clubs before earning fame and working with some of the world's greatest singers including Usher, Akon, Kelly Rowland and lots of others. The event is at Embassy nightclub this Saturday night. Buy the ticket and join the party and you will have a great time. And the next morning, while you may be recovering from a hangover, you will live happily ever after.

-The end-

(Oh, by the way, this event is sponsored by this cigarette or this alcoholic drink or this telecommunications company – buy their stuff too.)

See the story structure? I find it interesting that even if we were never taught formal fictional structure that somehow we find ourselves gravitating to writing stories as if we had been. I guess in a way, it's the classic thing to do and as long as we do what everyone else is doing (no matter how wrong it might be), then at least our jobs will be safe.

Famous management thinker Clayton Christenson refers to a lot of what we buy as doing "a job" such that people generally buy into a story because it does what they need the product to do, irrespective of any emotional attachment. Basically, for some things, we just can't be bothered to figure out how to do it ourselves so we buy something that settles the problem for us without having to endure the time and effort of doing it ourselves.

For example, many insurance companies in developing economies have made a business out of signing up clients to deposit 'x' amount each month just so the customers can prevent themselves from spending it on things they don't need. Effectively, people think they are buying an investment but the truth is they could just as easily deposit the money themselves and not give the insurance company free income if only they were a bit more disciplined. We "hire" the insurance company to make us disciplined.

But if we talk about *compelling* writing and storytelling, it makes sense that mixing around the order or even just focusing on one part of the story can give people a completely different perspective on what you are saying or selling. In other words, rather than "jobbing" our stories, we need to exercise a little bit of effort to find out how to make them compelling and that means leaving the comfort zone of classical storytelling.

I've always found that working backwards or hopping between stages works far better in order to get the story across. Here's why:

We live in an environment of either "information overload" or "mass ADD" (attention deficit disorder) – how you see the world is basically directly related to how cynical or optimistic you are. In any event, people generally don't take the time and effort to get past the first paragraph of your story unless it is really interesting and different. That means that it's not enough to have a little bit of everything there.

So what I suggest is a little different. We have to look at the story structure a bit differently:

1) **The Falling Action**: the falling action effectively is your "ideal scenario" where all of your major problems have been solved. It is what you aspire to be.

2) **The Introduction**: effectively the character development. By writing about the thinking behind what you are presenting, you are building a "we feel you dawg" case; that we understand and empathize with you

3) **The Rising Action**: this is where you talk about how your ideal situation was actually achieved in the product or service development.

As for the climax, let's just leave it out and as far as the triggering event, in the context of people's lives, invariably there are multiple triggering events, so being in sync with a person's character most of the time is better than appealing to just one instance of unhappiness.

In short, what you do is you catch people's attention by playing to their ideal sense of themselves. Then, you strengthen that argument by showing that you really "get them" by speaking to their current situation. Having locked in your credibility in your first two steps, now you can describe your product to your already captive audience. It's that simple.

The Big Bad Wolf

Ok, all of that sounds theoretical so let's try some examples to illustrate my point:

Little Red Riding Hood: Hero to All Little Girls

Little Red Riding Hood is a symbol of courage and determination. Together with her hunter friend, they vanquished a big bad wolf and showed that having a good heart and a sharp ax is far better than having big teeth. But Little Red Riding Hood was a girl born out of extreme hardship. Consider that her family owned no vehicle to get her safely through the forest, Grandma's house is a mere cabin and she lived in a rough area, filled with some very unsavory wolves. Thanks to the education that Little Red Riding Hood received from her local public school she developed basic survival skills and could run really, really fast. So really you should support your local public school.

Umm ... perhaps we should try something a bit more real world. Let's try to tell a story on the iPod, a device that completely transformed the music industry.

iPod: Your Music, Your Life, Your Freedom

Just imagine, now you can pick only the songs you love the most, the ones that tell your story, that bring you happiness each and every day, and now you can bring them anywhere! In the past, you bemoaned the fact that you had to buy entire albums filled with two great songs and ten crappy ones and still have to pay for them all. Imagine that you wanted to walk around and in order to bring only the songs you loved, you had to carry an entire backpack of music.

Well, the iPod was developed to completely right this wrong.

We developed this incredible platform where you could download only your favorite songs, all for a low price. We worked with the major studios to create this legally so that you wouldn't have to feel you were breaking the law. We developed this tiny instrument that fits in your back pocket weighing no more than a pack of playing cards. And your music is all right there!

Pretty compelling, right?[59]

The way you tell your story matters a lot. One technique that I can recommend is to focus on the aspiration first, then the reason why your product was created followed by a description of the product.

In sum, it's a simple process. Catch their attention, show that you can relate to them and then talk about how your product is awesome for them.

You'll be surprised by how effective these stories can be.

---

59 Thanks to the video power of Youtube and the prominence of blogs, for the first time, even smaller brands have the space/time/budget to tell this story in full.

TWELVE

THE BLUE PILL OR THE RED PILL

Creating Emotion In Your Story

MORPHEUS: Unfortunately, no one can be told what The Matrix is. You have to see it for yourself.
NEO: How?
MORPHEUS: Hold out your hands. This is your last chance. After this, there is no going back. You take the blue pill and the story ends. You wake in your bed and you believe whatever you want to believe. You take the red pill and you stay in Wonderland and I show you how deep the rabbit-hole goes. Remember that all I am offering is the truth. Nothing more.

- The Matrix (1999)[60]

---

60   The Matrix. Dir. The Wachowski Brothers. Warner Bros. Pictures, 1999.

Once you start empathizing with your customer as a storyteller, a whole range of benefits suddenly appears. People don't buy a product or a brand, they buy its meaning in their lives. More importantly, the entire way you approach the world will *completely* change. It's like Neo swallowing that red pill and seeing everything he thought was real disappearing before his very eyes to reveal an entirely different reality.

This four-dimensional view of the world (which becomes price, product, promotion and PEOPLE) suddenly gives you an insight that overcomes the bias that starts with the erroneous assumption of the "98% Rule". This makes sense because after all, even in 1970s, "gurus" like Peter Drucker correctly proclaimed that a company only exists to satisfy its customers.[61]

To get into the 4-D view, you can't just predict what customers would want from your products or brand, but why they *would not* want to patronize you. In some countries, human resources (HR) is more about figuring out the worst case scenario and working up from there. Marketers seem to be a more optimistic lot, but I think the HR people can teach us something. If you consider every customer to be a cynic who is too busy/risk-averse/comfortable/doesn't get it to switch to your brand or product, you start developing stories that make your product so compelling that it blows up the so-called "switching cost" into a million pieces for all but the most obstinate potential customers.

In my business for example, we say people don't merely buy a handbag, rather they buy a memory that the color or material awakens or an image of themselves using the handbag and how they will look. Capturing that image automatically makes people feel like you "get them".

---

61 The idea that a company "exists to satisfy its customers" surprisingly fell out of vogue over the last 40 years. Most people (and business schools) started to subscribe to the premise that a company's true purpose is "to make money for its shareholders". In fact, this latter view is a relatively new one and was 'hatched' in a 1970 essay penned by Nobel Prize-winning economist Milton Friedman. You can find the essay, entitled "The Social Responsibility of Business is to Increase its Profits" in the New York Times Magazine of September 13, 1970. In it, Friedman writes, "In a free-enterprise, private-property system, a corporate executive is an employee of the owners of the business. He has direct responsibility to his employers. That responsibility is to conduct the business in accordance with their desires, which generally will be to make as much money as possible while conforming to the basic rules of the society, both those embodied in law and those embodied in ethical custom." Friedman promotes the idea that conducting oneself as doing the best for society, or at least couching as such, is invariably something that's done to protect a business's self-interest. Thankfully, really good storytelling helps in that regard, but it turns out that helping out society makes for a really good story too.

The Ultimate Journey

An empathetic read on storytelling not only sears itself into the audience's collective consciousness, it tends to be unique to boot. Because no two people are exactly the same, your story can take a number of directions that will be unique to the audience.

Let's illustrate this through an example.

"Take this duffle bag made by American watch and accessories producer, Fossil. From a mere glance, this looks like a duffle bag and a pretty nice one at that. It is made of all leather and has a vintage look and costs about $300. It also can hold a lot of stuff."

In saying that, I've really just talked from my perspective. Probably any of a thousand other people would say the same thing and no work would have been necessary to write this product description.

However, if you look at the bag from a different perspective, you can transform the story.

"One problem with duffle bags is that because they are essentially free shapes, they are not the best to use if you want your clothes to remain stationary and folded. They are also not the best at holding their shape when other bags are piled on top of them (something which almost always happens whether in your car, a bus, a train or a plane). Yet you would like to bring a duffle with you instead of a suitcase because it's just less bulky.

The reason I know these things is because I've used duffle bags myself and I am starting to think "I wonder why my customers use or don't use duffle bags?"

This particular duffle bag has a kind of hard-framed top when it opens and closes, like a traditional doctor or lawyer's bag. When you pack this bag, it tends not to get scrunched down by other luggage very easily. Since the leather itself is quite thick, you would imagine that the bag would be a lot more stable overall. So if you wanted to go for a weekend trip or even a short business trip, your folded goods might actually stay in one piece, even if the bag got piled on. This, my friends, is why this duffle bag is great and totally worth $300. Oh, and it looks great too!" ☺

As soon as I make a description like this, I know my audience is going to think about weekend trips and it will elicit great memories for them. Or they'll think about all those times that they either were dissatisfied with a duffle bag or all the times they had to bring a bulky suitcase on a short business trip and think, "Yes! I always wondered why nobody thought of this before. It would make my life so much easier!" They might even play off the doctor or lawyer reference and feel the bag is more prestigious since it appeals to their desire to be seen as more distinguished.

The process looks something like this from bottom up.

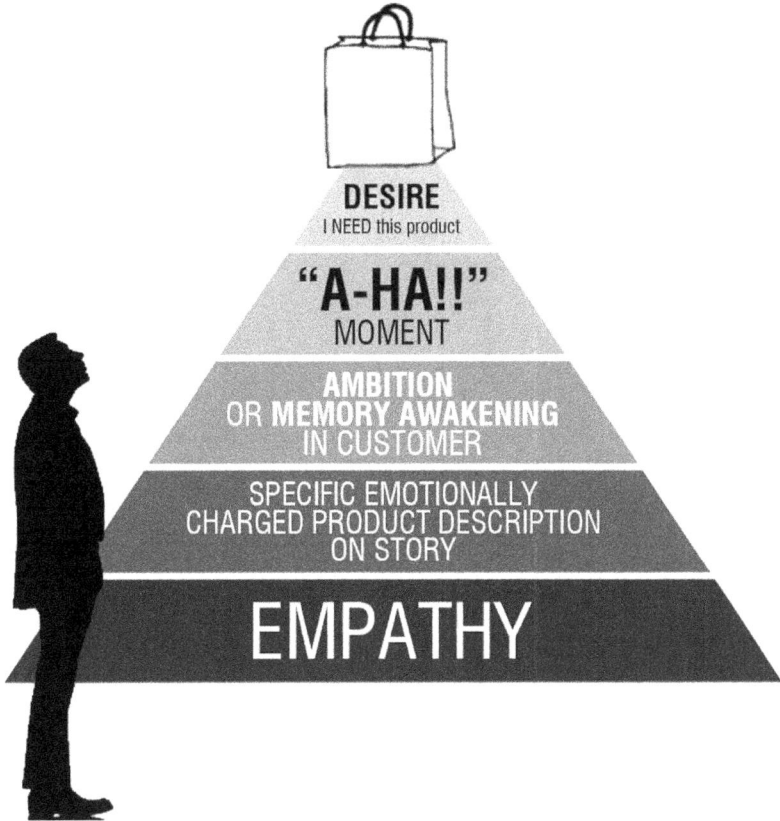

THE PATH TO THE PURCHASE

DESIRE
I NEED this product

"A-HA!!"
MOMENT

AMBITION
OR MEMORY AWAKENING
IN CUSTOMER

SPECIFIC EMOTIONALLY
CHARGED PRODUCT DESCRIPTION
ON STORY

EMPATHY

If you are doing a direct sales pitch it would lead to a very well-founded, concerted, strong recommendation to your customer as to why this product is the greatest thing *for them* since the invention of the wheel. This is a GREAT way to make friends at parties too.

The point is that pretty much everyone out there knows about customer segmentation. However, far fewer understand that empathetic story telling is a way of marketing to the few yet reaching the masses. It makes sense. After all, in a world of seven billion people, everyone is tired of being treated like just another number. Everyone *wants* to feel special, but how often is it that they *feel* it?

38 Special

I've always felt that the whole idea that "people buy products" is a little bit ridiculous. On the surface, it makes sense only from the standpoint that if you asked 100 people why they bought something, the first answer 99 of them would give you is: "I bought this because it looks nice." But actually, if you ask them further, what you discover is that the reason they *really* buy is not merely functional at all but rather very *emotional*. Their mouth is saying "I like this product because it's nice," but what their brain (or better put, their gut) is really telling them is "this product reminds me of something that I once experienced that brought me happiness."

Here's a slide I like to use when I train people on storytelling:

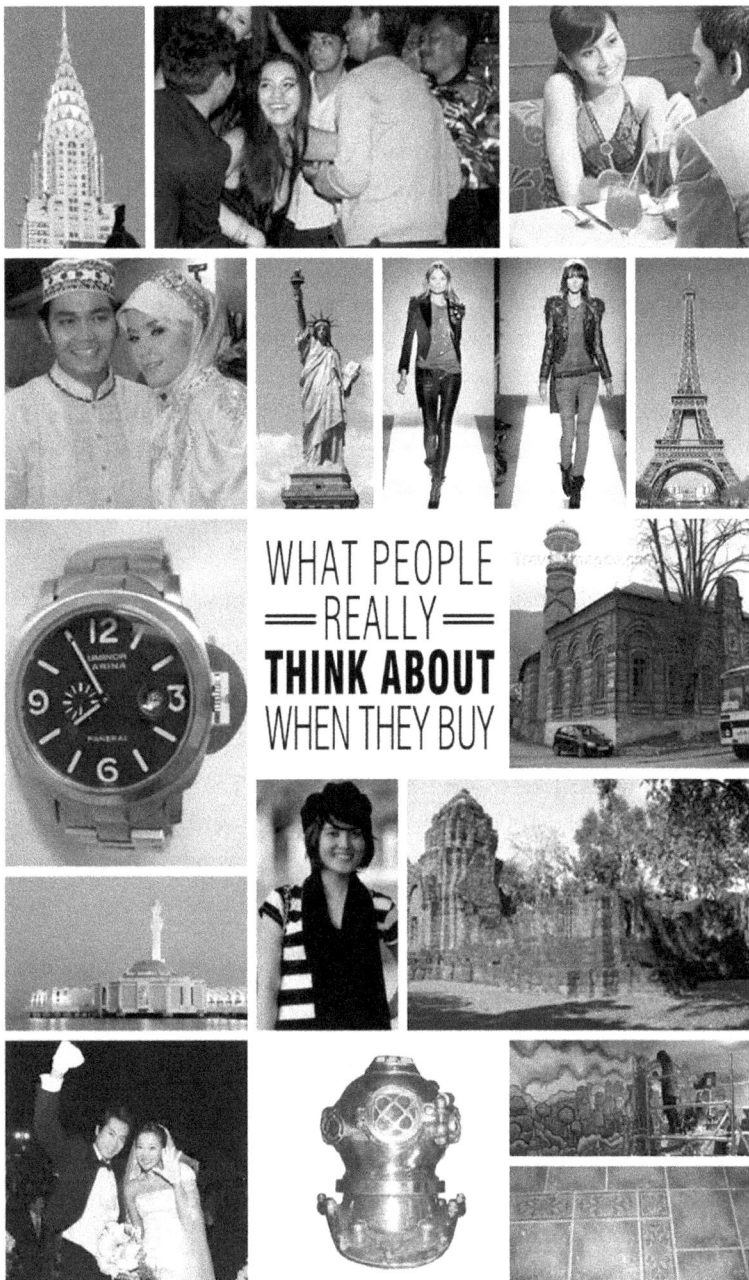

WHAT PEOPLE
===REALLY===
THINK ABOUT
WHEN THEY BUY

What you see in this slide is a collage of images but in general they refer to the internal aspirations that subconsciously go through people's heads when they see something.

- A place they remembered visiting
- A really happy time with their friends
- Something that was worn or used by someone they admire or like
- Something they saw in a movie
- Something related to architecture
- A time they were with their family and so on.

One aspect to looking at a graphic like this is that it forces you to question your own story. You can no longer assume, "I have a great product so everyone will like it." Rather, you would start to think, "My product's superiority isn't enough. What human emotion can I tap that will make this an undeniable benefit even to our biggest skeptics?"

I'd like to tell you about one particularly poignant moment in my own story-telling experience. Some years back, we were in the process of introducing a shift in our business to a "Purpose-Based Management" model. We sell watches and accessories from some of the biggest brands from around the world. We were trying to drill into our team this idea that there's a deeper reason why a person buys something.

As part of the exercise, we had asked all of our store managers to pick out a watch that they would like to wear for themselves. The prices of these products ranged between $100 and $600. Some of the products were best sellers while others were not so popular (e.g.: the $600 product). The only condition was that they had to start wearing this product as part of their work uniform and it was being given to them on loan (so they couldn't turn around and sell it).

We actually gave out the watches during the storytelling training. There was a catch though. In exchange for a free watch, we asked them to tell us why they picked that particular product. As part of the instructions, we told them that they could not talk about any function or material of the product.

The first nine people came up and told stories consisting of the very elements that we asked them not to include. In short, they had trouble connecting to the deeper meaning of the product. To them, the product still represented a nice color, a specific functionality or the brand itself.

And then the tenth person came up and told us a different story (by the way, he picked the most expensive product):

The Ultimate Journey

"I think there were a lot of products I could have chosen. To be honest, on the one hand, Emporio Armani means something to me in terms of its status. But the real reason I chose this watch was because it's blue. Actually, this blue reminds me of the suit I wore on my wedding day."

As he got to that last sentence, you could see his speaking pace slowing and in fact, he started tearing up as he was talking. In my years of training, this was one of the most magical moments I had experienced. He had, in under a minute, encapsulated the very essence of storytelling.

THIRTEEN

FEAR THE DEER

Managing Your Hype and the Cynical Customer

JOHN DOE: Realize, Detective, the only reason that I'm here right now is that I wanted to be.

MILLS: No. We...we would have gotten you eventually.

JOHN DOE: Oh, really? So what were you doing: biding your time? Toying with me? Allowing five "innocent" people to die until you felt like springing your trap? Tell me, what was the indisputable evidence you were going to use on me right before I walked up to YOU and put my hands in the air?

MILLS: John. Calm down. I seem to remember us knocking on your door.

JOHN DOE: Oh, that's right and I seem to remember breaking your face. You're only alive because I didn't kill you ... Remember that, Detective, every time you look in the mirror...at that face of yours, for the rest of your life. Or, I should say, for the rest of what life I've allowed you to have.

MILLS: Sit back...sit back, you fucking freak! Shut your fucking mouth! You're no messiah. You're a movie of the week. You're a fucking t-shirt. At best.

- Se7en (1995)[62]

---

62   Se7en. Dir. David Fincher. New Line Cinema, 1995.

In "Se7en", as Agents Mills and Somerset are driving the mysterious killer, John Doe, to a remote area to find the final two bodies in John's great plan, a heated argument ensues about whether these crimes will be remembered long after the case is solved. It's an interesting dialogue because it demonstrates how we often perceive our own actions, brands or products in a way that is much more impressive than how others view us. In short, our bias leads us to believe our own hype a bit too much.

In early 2011, I had an interesting conversation with a college business professor. The topic turned to tablets and he began raving about the just-released Blackberry Playbook. His theory was that while the machine wasn't perfect, everyone would eventually gravitate to it because Blackberry had cutting edge security protection and that's what was most important to everyone those days.

Well, it turns out that not only was security not the only thing on people's minds but the machine itself was just poorly conceived.[63] It didn't even push email, something rather inexplicable since Apple, Samsung and a host of others had mastered that rather simple task years earlier. Given such basic failings, the Playbook never had a chance; it couldn't possibly live up to its hype.

The $40 Steak and Fries Test

When I was traveling to Europe as a student, I developed something I called "The $40 Steak and Fries Test". But let me start at the beginning.

In the summer of 1994, I traveled to West Africa as part of a Canadian International Development Agency co-sponsored group working with students to train them on how to develop campus organizations. This was my first really exotic overseas trip and of course, one of the first things I had to get used to was the food. At the time, while you could get Coke and a few other things, there weren't any McDonald's or Pizza Huts or anything really familiar. Our only options were small restaurants serving local fare or some local interpretation of foreign foods.

Meat was of course an interesting proposition on account that you couldn't simply run out to your local supermarket and grab a fresh Grade A sirloin or anything. Quite the opposite. I recall in one restaurant ordering goat stew and sitting

---

63 You could argue that the exact opposite is true. In today's hyper-connected society, one could argue that in order to not get lost in the anonymity of 7 billion people, today's global citizen actually eschews security and *wants* to be found.

patiently waiting for my meal until about 10 minutes later we heard the sound of goats bleating outside. The goat stew arrived shortly after. I was no longer hungry.

For a nice Canadian boy like me, it was even hard to eat poultry after seeing live chickens roaming the campus grounds where we stayed. In fact, livestock were everywhere (even sometimes riding on buses with us). I started cutting back on my meat consumption for the rest of the summer.

On the way back to Canada, we had a weeklong stopover in Europe and I decided to make a quick detour from Schiphol Airport in Amsterdam to Brussels, thinking that getting another stamp in my passport would be fun.[64] Not having anything other than "fresh from the backyard" meat for two and a half months had gotten me really hyped up for *steak et frites* (steak and fries), one of the signature dishes of any visit to Belgium and I swear for the entire trip from Amsterdam to Belgium, I was literally salivating at the chance to eat this delectable meal.[65]

When I arrived in Brussels, I found a hostel, dropped off my stuff and immediately ran to the nearest place offering steak-et-frites. Although the dish cost the equivalent of $40, a considerable sum of money for a "poor" student like me who had grown accustomed to $1 meals in Africa, I figured it must be worth it and thought nothing of making the order. After all, you have to try steak and fries in a French-inspired European country at least once before you die. Minutes later, the dish arrived. It looked good and then I took my first bite.

But something strange happened "on the way to heaven". As I took my first bite, then my second and so on, I became increasingly aware that this meal was not 40 times better than anything I had eaten in Canada, the US or even in West Africa. In fact, the whole thing seemed much ado about nothing. I started feeling an immense sense of "Buyer's Remorse" and wondered what that money could have been better used for. In fact, the perceived value of that meal was not only less than $40; it was probably actually closer to *minus-$40!*

From this experience I created the $40 Steak and Fries Test, the idea that when you are anticipating something, it often doesn't live up to your expectations. You can hype something up so much that it might even get to the point where there is no way that it could *ever* live up to your expectations.

---

64 It turns out that the border between the Netherlands and Belgium is invisible. No stamp, no fun. A decade and a half later, I had the same experience crossing from Germany to Austria. This time I was at least just looking for a border instead of a stamp. So Europe has vastly disappointed me, twice.

65 Or so I was told.

That said, in a few cases, I've experienced things that *did* deserve the hype and where I felt I could have paid many times more and still felt satisfied. Some examples of this included watching my first Cleveland Indians baseball game, my first iPad purchase and the 2013 Swedish House Mafia "One Last Tour" concert, for which I shelled out quite a bit of cash.

Surely all of us have similar experiences where something either passed or failed the $40 Steak and Fries Test (or something akin to it).

Now in truth, in the Brussels case and all the other cases I've just mentioned, the inflation of the "perceived value" of the purchase/experience was self-inflicted. In each case, the desire came not from anyone marketing it to me but rather from my own interests, hobbies and that evil red "buy light" in my head. This is basically what happens to the so-called "early adopters" of any product.

Walking the Walk

In contrast, those who buy into something during the mass adoption stage of a product are generally influenced by other factors, many of which are driven by marketers. These can take many forms, including extensive media coverage, their own claims or some large PR event staged for the product.

In the next chapter, I'll talk about the "Rule of ST" which posits that if you want to sell something, the easiest way to make people take notice is by attaching a superlative to the product.

Still, before you even get to superlatives, it's best to test if your product can live up to the hype. In fact, overhyping something can be one of the most dangerous things you can do. This is why Blackberry's hype of the Playbook helped to nearly plunder the company within just a few months of its release.

In March 2013, Sam Grobart wrote a great article about Samsung for Bloomberg Businessweek.[66] He mentioned that while Samsung is one of the heaviest promoters in the world of their products, there was a point when the company was more circumspect in how it viewed even its own quality.

Two paragraphs in particular stood out for me:

---

66   A full copy of the article can be found at www.businessweek.com/articles/2013-03-28/how-samsung-became-the-worlds-no-dot-1-smartphone-maker

"Such striving for efficiency and excellence wasn't always a priority. In 1995, Chairman Lee (ed: Lee Kun Hee, Chairman of Samsung) was dismayed to learn that cell phones he gave as New Year's gifts were found to be inoperable. He directed underlings to assemble a pile of 150,000 devices in a field outside the Gumi factory. More than 2,000 staff members gathered around the pile. Then it was set on fire. When the flames died down, bulldozers razed whatever was remaining. "If you continue to make poor-quality products like these," Lee Keon Hyok recalls the chairman saying, "I'll come back and do the same thing." [67]

"The lesson stuck. In May 2012, three weeks before the new Galaxy S III was to be shipped, a Samsung customer told the company that the back covers for the smartphone looked cheaper than the demo models shown to clients earlier. 'He was right,' says DJ Lee, the marketing chief of Samsung Mobile. 'The grain wasn't as fine on the later models.' There were 100,000 covers in the warehouse with the inferior design, as well as shipments of the assembled devices waiting at airports. This time, there would be no bonfire—all 100,000 covers, as well as those on the units at the airports, were scrapped and replaced."

An interesting follow-up to this was a presentation by one of Samsung's Southeast Asia-based marketing managers in September 2011 when describing the first iteration of the Galaxy Tab and how they created demand to the point that they had a big line of people waiting to get the first machines.

The manager admitted that the Galaxy Tab was a relatively "ugly" machine compared to the iPad and that they had to push demand instead of pulling in converts as the iPad had successfully done from the time it was first announced in late 2010. In order to get customers, Samsung had to rely on a message that focused on the functionality of the machine while offering discounts in order to entice customers to give it a chance. He even related how the company drove the hype up to such an extent that the first non-working prototype was auctioned off at a charity event for more than 10 times the price of an actual working version.

Over time, Samsung was able to considerably improve the look, feel and quality of its Tabs.[68] Eighteen months later, after the company felt reasonably certain that they could stand toe-to-toe with Apple, they decided to make their big splash at

---

67 "The Samsung Era" by Sam Grobart, Bloomberg Businessweek, April 2013.

68 Which makes sense since they invented the touch-sensitive glass that made the iPad and iPhone such revolutionary products. They even initially supplied the glass to Apple.

the 2012 Super Bowl with an advertisement for the Galaxy Note lampooning Apple fans' tendency to camp out in front of Apple stores for new products.

While the ad didn't necessarily resonate with many on account of the fact that a stylus just isn't all that sexy,[69] you could see that Samsung was starting to get comfortable with the idea that their products were actually developing a better screen, a better size and a competitive operating system.

By the time the Tab 3 hit the market in 2013, the company was no longer selling based on price and me-too-ness but was actively promoting the revolutionary aspects of their product (the clearest display ever, better camera, etc.) and the emotional aspects of the product.[70] They had realized that in order to tell a story, they had to revolutionize the offering. In time, even some diehard Apple users started gravitating to Samsung's products.

Samsung's story finally matched its hype.

Jeff Bezos' Crystal Ball

Amazon is an excellent case of a company that developed its story from within rather than pumping up the hype first. When the company started in the late 90s, e-commerce was still in its infancy and traditional booksellers like Barnes & Noble and Borders still ruled the roost with their bricks-and-mortar model.

Bezos certainly knew at that point that he could not offer the same level of choice or the physical environment as established players. True enough, in the beginning, Amazon wasn't the best in the field. However, Bezos had caught onto the incredible value of bringing order to the paradox of choices consumers faced in choosing books to read.

After all, even an avid reader is invariably a prisoner of scarcity; they have neither the time nor the money to read every book on the market. One drawback to the traditional bookstore was the difficulty in finding an exact book suited to your interests. For sure, you could easily find bestsellers, but if you were looking for books that appealed to a specific mood or topic, the physical bookstore format was not ideal.

---

69 Something which Steve Jobs so aptly pointed out (no pun intended) in his introduction to the first iPhone back at MacWorld in January 2007.
70 And having NBA star Lebron James back anything is a sure way to benefit from the Midas Touch. The guy is unstoppable on or off the court.

The Ultimate Journey

Bezos was one of a few leaders who was willing to make a long-term investment at a loss with an eye toward "building the story" for the future. Perhaps the most explicit expression of that desire came in his 1997 letter to shareholders:

"Amazon.com passed many milestones in 1997 … But this is Day 1 for the internet and, if we execute well, for Amazon.com. Today, online commerce saves customers money and precious time. Tomorrow, through personalization, online commerce will accelerate the very process of discovery. Amazon.com uses the internet to create real value for its customers and, by doing so, hopes to create an enduring franchise, even in established and large markets." [71]

If you read this letter carefully, you can see that Bezos had his eye on the larger prize. In 1997, he knew that he was a good player and had a compelling offer to customers, but that the product was very much a work in progress. For Bezos, personalization and a focused determination on having the best level of customer ease and service and most timely deliveries in the future was going to make Amazon one of the most incredible shopping experiences in human history. You could see this in a later paragraph in that letter.

"From the beginning, our focus has been on offering our customers compelling value. The web was, and still is, the World Wide Wait. Therefore, we set out to offer customers something they simply could not get in any other way and began serving them with books. We brought them much more selection than was possible in a physical store (our store would now occupy 6 football fields) and presented it in a useful, easy-to-search and easy-to-browse format in a store open 365 days a year, 24 hours a day. We maintained a dogged focus on improving the shopping experience, and in 1997 substantially enhanced our store. We now offer customers gift certificates, 1-Click Shopping, and vastly more reviews, content, browsing options and recommendation features. We dramatically lowered prices, further increasing customer value. Word of mouth remains the most powerful customer acquisition tool we have and we are grateful for the trust our customers have placed in us. Repeat purchases and word of mouth have combined to make Amazon.com the market leader in online bookselling."

In a 2013 Shareholder Letter, Bezos hearkens back to the 1997 letter as a story that is still being acted on. In effect, this letter *is* the Amazon story.

The interesting thing about Amazon is that they actually do very little outside advertising and in the early days, the company focused predominately on the

---

71   Taken from Jeff Bezos' Letter to Shareholders from Amazon's 1997 Annual Report.

affiliate-based arrangements in order to bring traffic to their site. So you could argue that Amazon's story has been largely internal since the outset and they've achieved the external story by the simple execution of their business.

This isn't necessarily an uncommon strategy for the world's best companies. Increasingly, the most sought after products and brands are those in which other people tell the story to their friends and acquaintances for free despite never having formally heard the company tell its story. Yet interestingly, what often happens is that the external story is identical because the company had a clear internal story from the beginning and worked toward that. Usually this story has been communicated either through the company's mission or through other tools, such as Bezos' shareholder letter.

One could say that a story could be interchanged with a "vision" and largely this is true. In many respects, a company that is simply "there to compete" can never tell a compelling story because it has no vision. On the other hand, a brand with a compelling vision tends to come out with products and a brand that has a tremendously resonating story. This really plays into the idea that for most companies, you build your products around your story and not the other way around.

In the end, it's ok to hype. Marketing is partly about creating hype around your product. However, for those who are playing a "long game", a spoonful of humility is greater than a container-full of hype. This is when it becomes important to view things as a cynical customer.

The Cynical Customer Method

One of the most important tools I can share is the concept of the "cynical customer".[72] This builds on the concepts of empathy and relatability that I discussed earlier.

---

72 I have a few rules on how to differentiate between a cynical and an impossible customer.

Rule 1: Both customers are bored of sales messages, but the cynical customer is one who is looking for a story that makes sense and isn't opposed to buying.
Rule 2: A cynical customer is looking for a fair relationship, an impossible customer is looking for a one-sided relationship that ignores business reality
Rule 3: A cynical customer is practical. They know that there are things that a brand can and cannot economically do. An impossible customer ignores economic reality.
Rule 4: A cynical customer accepts that they don't know all the facts and wants to be educated. An impossible customer assumes that a salesperson is nothing more than a pawn and doesn't even want to hear them.
Rule 5: Both customers are jaded from having been lied to before.

The Ultimate Journey

If you believe the theory of the "Inverse 98% Rule", that is, most customers actually do not relate to or believe in your brand and the hype, then it's very important to double-check everything you put out. The key to the Cynical Customer Method is to assume that people will <u>not</u> believe anything you put out. If you try to empathize with the cynical customer, you'll find yourself making criticisms to even the fundamental aspects of your product and message. Make no mistake; this is absolutely super-productive since it pushes you to be genuine in what you communicate to the public.

If you hold your communications to a higher standard by writing for people who would be dubious of your claims, it will challenge you to refine your message so that even cynics would say, "Well, I can see where you're coming from." They still might not agree in all cases, but your story would become better for your existing customers and more plausible for a certain segment of non-customers who are willing to be swayed.

This does not mean to entirely disregard all of your internal hype. It just forces to you to sharpen it. Keep in mind again that there are two kinds of non-customers out there: people who would never buy from you and people who don't currently buy from you but might be convinced if you "hit a chord" with your message. When we talk about the cynical customer, we're talking only about the latter group.

The method is very simple. Simply read over what you've written and ask these questions:

1. Do I have actual proof that the claims about my product or brand are true?
2. Under what circumstances would a person have need for or find my product particularly useful?
3. Is that reflected here?

If the answer to any of these questions is "no", it's probably time to re-write or adjust. If you can confidently say "yes" to all of these questions, you can press the send button and feel pretty good about what you're putting out there.

Key Take-Aways

The evolution of Samsung and Amazon from "me-too" product to stand-alone best on the market (albeit with some dispute) is instructive of how you communicate when you really don't have the best product. The Cynical Customer Method helps you to further fine tune your message so you're putting the right "temperature" on your story.

Lesson 1: Don't Overhype

There's a tendency for marketers who subscribe to the "98% Rule" to shout out a sub-standard product to the rafters. This is one of the most foolish things that you can do. One of the most important elements of storytelling is your ability to not just tell a story, but to allow others to actually live it when they make an investment in your brand. If you sell them the "greatest product ever" and it breaks the first time they use it, your life is about to enter a whole world of pain, particularly in the super-fast, super-connected social media age. If one bad customer experience used to mean 10 lost customers, today that multiple is probably closer to a few thousand.[73]

One basic character trait that good parents teach their children from a young age is honesty. When you enter the marketing or storytelling business, that's definitely not the time to check your honesty at the door. In fact, if anything, Samsung's experiences (both good and bad) show that it's better for a company to build its message in step with the quality of its product.

Lesson 2: Build Your Product into Your Story, Not the Other Way Around

It's very rare that a company enters an industry and is immediately hailed as the best. Perhaps this happens less than 1% of the time, partly due to the fact that it takes time to perfect a product and partly since there is almost no industry in which there are not pre-existing competitors with well-entrenched strengths.

Since almost no strategy can be precisely "cut and pasted" from a previous experience, you always need time. As such, storytelling has to start from within the company rather than directly to the consumer. If you currently have a mediocre product (or better to say "a work in progress"), you'll need to strive to develop the story. Instead of shouting superlatives, your message can become "We are striving to be and will eventually succeed to be the X-st". This means that you build your culture perhaps through a manifesto (we'll discuss manifestos later) or other internal communications like your training, your internal newsletters and even the tone in which you write emails.

In truth, this idea of mission and story-based management is probably one of the hardest skills for anyone to master, especially when they are "on the clock" with a new venture that will initially be cash-draining or where expectations are high to deliver immediately. On the plus side, by keeping the message internal, it encourages companies to manage their cash first until they can fully "earn" their story.

---

73 Just see what a bad review on TripAdvisor can do to a hotel.

FOURTEEN

THE GREATEST SHOW ON EARTH

Competition and The Power of Superlatives

ZIDLER: I mean the show will be ... a magnificent, opulent, tremendous, stupendous, gargantuan bedazzlement! A sensual ravishment! Spectacular, Spectacular! No words in the vernacular can describe this great event. You'll be dumb with wonderment. Returns are fixed at ten percent. You must agree that's excellent. And on top of your fee ...

ALL: You'll be involved artistically. So exciting, the audience will stomp and cheer. So delighting, it will run for fifty years. So exciting, the audience will stomp and cheer. So delighting, it will run for fifty years!

- Moulin Rouge (2001)[74]

---

74   Moulin Rouge. Dir. Buz Luhrmann. 20th Century Fox, 2001.

At the beginning of the epic Buz Luhrman film "Moulin Rouge", the director of a cabaret company, Harold Zidler, pitches the latest performance, "Spectacular, Spectacular" to a financier. What you see in the quote is how Zidler pitches to the financier's innate desire to be a part of something massive. Eventually, Zidler succeeds in doing so and the show gets financed, albeit with fatal consequences.

We would all like to think our stories are the greatest and most unique that anyone has ever heard. Sadly, we often find to our disappointment that our story is just like dozens, hundreds or even thousands of others out there.

Let me give you an illustration. I once had a girlfriend whom I liked very much (my friends still ask me why) and whom I was with for more than two years. Being relatively new to romance, I was obviously very excited and felt that this was "the one" (ok, stop rolling your eyes and let me finish). To me, everything was new and exciting about being in a serious relationship.

To a large extent, the reason why it lasted so long was that I was truly enamored with being in a relationship and grappled with the fear, one nearly everyone at some point confronts, that I would never find another partner like her. Somehow, even without writing it down at the time, I kept track of everything that happened to us together.

Eventually, she went overseas to study. After a few months, I left my business and moved into my parents' home and got a pretty dead-end job just to be closer to her. Not more than six months later, she told me she wanted to break up.

I was shattered. I had no idea how something that felt so right had gone so wrong. In a fit of self-pity (or insanity – I can't tell which), I started recounting the entire relationship into something that I gave some moronic name like the "Love Chronicles" or "The Chronicles of a Broken Heart" (ok, it definitely was insanity).

And so I wrote … and I wrote … and I wrote. I chronicled the whole thing. By the end, it had reached 210 heart-wrenching pages.

I was actually quite impressed with my feat in that 1) I had never written a full-length book before and 2) I swear I had managed to remember at least 900 of the 1,000 or so days that we had been together. The 200-odd pages were full of details about hope gained and lost, happy times and bitter arguments and of course the despair that such a promising relationship had failed so miserably.

And then suddenly something occurred to me …

I realized probably 500 million other men had almost certainly ridden a similar emotional roller coaster of failed romance. Lost in my self-pity, it dawned on me that this had at some point happened to EVERYONE!

In truth, my story wasn't so special after all when confronted with the reality of millions just like it. I thought about it for a moment, locked the file in my computer and eventually deleted it.

And that, my friends, is how I got over the heartache of my first serious broken relationship.

The Ultimate Story

The Old Testament is the most widely read and probably the world's very first storybook. Aside from being a fantastic and compelling read, it's actually the perfect reference point to understand the importance of competition in storytelling.

For anyone who has the read the Bible, you'll surely know the story of Adam and Eve. They lived a blissful life in the Garden of Eden until that dastardly serpent managed to convince Eve into thinking the fruit on the Forbidden Tree was somehow worth trying.[75] That serpent can be seen as either the best salesperson or the most devious snake oil fraudster of all time (pardon the pun).

So in the beginning (if you follow the Bible – and if you don't, just run with me here), there were only two people on the planet. If you wanted to tell a great human story, Adam and Eve were it. They could be sitting under a tree all day flicking apple seeds and you would have to say that their story was riveting. Of course, you had no choice. It was either "Adam and Eve's Wonderful Life" or you were going story-free for the day.

Flash forward a few thousand (or million – depending on your predisposition) years to the present. We are now beyond seven billion people on this planet. I'm going to bet you that a story about Adam and Eve collecting apple seeds isn't going to cut it anymore in the annals of epic human dramas.

Adam and Eve in the 21st Century

So, what changed? Well, there's a lot of competition out there and a lot of good stories. This partly explains why my depraved love story was ultimately not worthy of publication.

---

75   While popular imagery has given many the impression that the fruit is an apple, there's no consensus among religious scholars about exactly what kind of fruit was on the tree. Some say it's a fig, others, a sheaf of wheat. Still, people remember the basic lesson, which just goes to show you that truly great stories preserve their key lessons incredibly well, even though they might mutate over time.

Interestingly, it is possible that never before in recorded history has it been so advantageous as it is now to be unique. In the 16th century, Nicolas Copernicus came up with a "crazy" theory that perhaps the universe did not revolve around the earth. He was so afraid of being labeled an outcast for his unique view of the universe that he kept the idea to himself for more than a decade before finally gathering up the courage to publish his story. And what a story it was, laying the ground for some of the greatest scientific discoveries of all time. Today it seems inconceivable to us that anyone could ever have though that the earth was the center of the universe.

Over the years, people have been labeled as crazy for thinking differently; for thinking that a machine could fly through the air or that we could transfer voices and pictures through a wooden box or (more controversially) that UFOs could be hovering over a vast expanse of the New Mexico desert. Whether such "deviant" thinking was in the end proven correct or not, the defining connection between all of these stories is that they were largely dismissed at first by a disbelieving public that had neither the access to information sources nor the ability to see anything outside their own town for much of their life.

And yet today, we look at a wide range of opinions and sources via the internet, we watch wildly insane rumors crossing cyberspace or "shock TV". We seem to enjoy listening to these stories and wondering whether there's a semblance of truth to any of them. In the internet age, anything and everything is possible. As a result, it seems that everyone has a story and it's becoming increasingly likely to get drowned out.

Too often we come across marketers who are so focused on their own universe that they think the rest of the world must care about what they have to say. They find it inconceivable that everyone else doesn't share the same intractable emotional attachment to their products.

There are certain products that undoubtedly maintain a strong emotional hold on us, not simply because of what they are but also because of how they contributed to a greater memory or aspiration that we had. Yes, we can get emotional about a car because it might have been our first major personal investment, a sign that we had personally 'arrived' at a certain status, or perhaps it had transported us on a truly memorable trip, or maybe it was something in which we practically lived (ideal for those people who live in cities with horrific traffic).

It's possible you feel emotionally attached to certain items if the store that sold them had been therapeutic to you during your stressful times. Some people get a buzz out of going to Victoria's Secret or Uniqlo while others perhaps just remember trudging home after a long night of partying and dropping in to H&M in midtown Manhattan to pick up some new clothes so they can just roll into work without ever having gone home (and yes, it does happen). It's possible you may have a special emotional attachment to In-N-Out Burger after waiting outside overnight in sub-zero temperatures just so you could be the first in line for their grand opening in your town.

Still, for most people, their attachment to the vast majority of products is somewhere between "it's ok" to "what are we talking about here?"

There's one other element at play here; that with increased competition, it is rare to be the only product in any given marketplace. In most cases, product lines have become commoditized to the point that either you have the clear benefit of being cheaper than the competition or you have a maybe 10% differentiation from everyone else in the market. Rarely are you so remarkably different that you could put your product next to all others and people would just *know* your product is special.

For everyone else, you are basically stuck fighting a battle for scorched earth. While it's great that you have a marketing department or agency that can make a funny commercial or a viral video, in the end, this is still just a shell game in which you can attract people's attentions for a while.

But look at the greatest companies and their stories are really compelling. That absolutely undeniable attraction comes from their adherence to what I call "The Law of ST".

ST'ing It!

Everyone knows that journalists follow the 5 Ws when researching a story but while who, what, when and where are very important questions and make up the body of the story, a lot of people miss out on the why of the story; as in "Why is this story so important?"

Hence we bring up the "Law of ST". If you want to know why your story is so important, just figure out which "ST" word can be attached to what you do.

By "ST" words, I mean superlatives. Those are words that describe an extreme point in any range of options. Here are some good superlatives that you should always keep in your personal vocabulary:
- Best/Worst
- Highest/Lowest

- Biggest/Smallest
- First/Last
- Most/Least
- Tallest/Shortest
- Hardest/Easiest
- Latest/Newest/Oldest
- Prettiest
- Cheapest

When I was writing this chapter, I was thinking to myself, "I can't believe I'm writing this. This is the easiest (there's my 'ST' word) thing that anyone could ever imagine. I mean a kindergarten student would probably know this."

Feeling the Beat

Yet surprisingly, only a small percentage of people I come across ever think about their writing in this way. In fact, if you read a lot of press releases out there, they are surprisingly missing these 'ST' words entirely. It's as if they think that as a reporter or a customer, you have nothing better to do than to read a full story about something that's an "also-ran".

As I mentioned earlier, for many years, I was editing a watch magazine for my company. After a while I got a bit depressed because it seemed like every story was merely a slight variation from every other story. Perhaps because of that, most casual readers of timepiece magazines simply skip the stories and just make a beeline to the pictures.

Over the years, I came to a realization that the stories from most brands really were just product pitches of very ordinary pieces. In the luxury world, occasionally you get unique pieces that are grounded in a very strong historical story. Those are cool to read. Sadly, 90% of products are not like that and as a result, crafting a vivid story for these products is as difficult as squeezing water from a stone.

A few years back, I wrote an editorial piece to summarize one of the timepiece fairs entitled "More Blue Than Pink" in which I described my disappointment at how few "real stories" were actually emerging from the industry. It seemed as if everyone was recycling old models and presenting them as new.

Because we were supported by ads from the industry, I was careful not to sound too negative. Still, I just couldn't bring myself to promote the fairs as being overly innovative when I knew that was truly not the case. Since I just couldn't believe a spin story, I couldn't write one either.

One thing about superlatives is that you have to use them with a "straight face". In other words, you actually have to *believe* in what you are saying most of the time (although if you are a time-honored brand or paying significant ad dollars, then you can say whatever you want and people *have* to cover you).

When you write for branding, it's a lot like being the "big man on campus". These BMOCs are not necessarily the most handsome or beautiful, they aren't necessarily the smartest and they may not be the most outgoing, but there's a certain aura about them. They *know* they are special and everyone feels it.

This is entirely different from the person who is actively pandering to get attention and invariably ends up being the one who gets hazed or used because they just *seem desperate.*

Showing Your True Colors

You need to have confidence when you write and knowing your "ST" from the onset is what gives you that aura. Let me give you an example in real life:

I've been working for a distributor of fashion brands for many years and when we started, we were well behind our main competitor. They outsold us at a rate of something like ten to one. In the early years, we tried to ape our main competitor, we placed outlets near theirs, we went on sale whenever they did, we tried to build our stores to be just like theirs and we got stressed every time they did any kind of promotion.

About four years into the business we got sick of playing second fiddle. We had some amazing brands with great prices and we felt we had the best products. We knew our designs were better than theirs.

We decided to reframe the story. We started building a brand story where we leveraged off the fact that we had the most creative, best designs and we had the fairest prices. So we built the story around our strengths.

By year five, we had already exceeded our competitor, who by then had to resort to monthly discounting just to maintain their market. Whenever they took a competitive action, we just shrugged it off and stuck to our story and kept adding value so our "best" just kept getting better and better.

Over time, the story became compelling to customers and mall owners alike. They could not deny that there was something special about our business model and the way that we provided dignity to customers and the marketplace in a way our competitors did not. It doesn't mean it put an end to competition, but it certainly paved our way to high double-digit growth for six years, a streak interrupted only in 2009 due to the financial crisis.

So here's how you start creating your "ST-ory":

<u>Step 1:</u> Ask what is it about what you do that is better and different from everyone else?

This is the toughest part of the exercise because you need to separate yourself from your company loyalties and take a good hard look at what is absolutely, undeniably true. The biggest mistake you can make is to do this with a bias.

<u>Step 2:</u> Ask what is the impact of that unique quality that you have.

Once you've done these two steps then you can flow your story from there. And make sure you use "ST" words in all of your writing since superiority or differentiation is most sought-after by reporters.

It's amazing that when you ask people what is their version of "Spectacular, Spectacular", they just seem to stutter their words. There's no substitute for taking a little time to know your true story. "ST" words just get you there that much faster.

THE ORBIT PHASE:
NEW WAYS TO MAINTAIN YOUR STORY

FIFTEEN

MANIFEST DESTINY
The Art of Writing a Great Company Manifesto

MELVIN: Okay, now. I got a great compliment for you, and it's true.
CAROL: I'm so afraid you're about to say something awful.
MELVIN: Don't be pessimistic. It's not your style... Okay. Here I go. Clearly a mistake. I've got this...ailment. My doctor, this shrink I used to go to all the time... he says in 50-60% of the cases a pill really helps. Now I hate pills. Very dangerous things, pills. I am using the word hate here with pills. Hate 'em. Anyway I never took them...then that night when you came over and said that you would never... well, you were there, you know what you said. And here's the compliment. That next morning, I took the pills.
CAROL: I'm not quite sure how that's a compliment for me.
MELVIN: You make me want to be a better man.
CAROL: That's maybe the best compliment of my life.

- As Good As It Gets (1997)[76]

---

76   As Good As It Gets. Dir. James L. Brooks. TriStar Pictures, 1997.

Ah…good old Jack Nicholson. If ever there was ever a curmudgeon in a movie, Melvin Udall is it. A rich, aging novelist with a serious case of obsessive-compulsive disorder falls for a woman who forces him to not only confront his own feelings and fears but to open himself to sharing his life with others. For close to two hours, Melvin goes around putting down other people and separating himself from the rest of the world that he desperately wants to join, even if only to start a relationship with a local waitress, Carol Connelly. And yet, somehow, unwarily, and against his greatest fears, he manages to find the words that have eluded him all this time, simply by being honest with those around him. In short, he shows his true colors in the barest way possible.

In the old days, when brands started up, they were generally named after their owners, people who worked out of one particular location and actually took an active role in everything that came out of their company. Coco Chanel started off by making hats. Levi Strauss found ways to drive rivets into everyday work pants so gold nuggets wouldn't fall out of the pockets. Watchmakers like Jean-Marc Vacheron and Antoine LeCoultre set up small workshops where they would work on specific requests by customers. Louis Vuitton Malletier started off making trunks in a small house on Rue Neuve des Capucines in Paris. The list goes on and on.

One thing was common. When people talked about a brand, it represented the basic character of their founder. Over the years, as enterprises became bigger, that sense of connection between the founder's basic human personality was lost under a faceless corporate facade.

For most of the 20th century in particular, and particular its latter decades, most companies focused on what they provided to customers and tended to gloss over the deeper human cultural aspects of their organizations. This made sense. After all, most people aspired to join conglomerates or large publicly listed companies that made their name by their size and products as opposed to their internal culture.

In the late 90s and early part of the 21st century, something happened that changed all of that. In the late 90s, the technology boom started in earnest in the United States. Rather than joining companies that might have had thousands or even tens of thousands of employees, highly skilled people started joining companies that started from scratch. These companies lacked the resources to pay their teams with top dollars and instead offered only stock options and the opportunity to do something great in the world.

The Ultimate Journey

As a result, not only were company founders more visible than they had been for decades, but the mission of a company in the world once again came into vogue. In order to be heard by the public or even venture capitalists, companies had to re-focus to understand why they really mattered to society. Not only did they have to explain internally, but for the first time, they also had to share it explicitly to outsiders.

In the first decade of the 21st century, as we passed through various stages of social meeting places ranging from Friendster to MySpace to Facebook and Twitter, people started to develop their knowledge of their friends, family and the companies they frequented via their social media profiles. For the first time, we could find out everything about celebrities, politicians, corporate leaders and famous athletes directly from them and from people talking about them.

We had entered the Age of Transparency.

In this chapter, I'll talk about how the manifesto has gone from a simple rallying point to now becoming a useful (and in some cases integral) part of a brand's storytelling and can be seamlessly integrated into your brand's journey.

Letting it All Hang Out

One of the problems I've often noticed about new companies is that when they are very small, it's relatively easy to maintain a consistent message. In many cases, founders or their closest lieutenants take hold of the social media and storytelling reins and communicate directly to the world. But at a certain point, a company gets bigger, the founders get busy and they can no longer manage the day-to-day messages that reinforce how the story of the company's culture is told. This gets left to other people who might be either junior employees or more experienced professionals who came from other organizations and already have "a system" for talking about a company. Over time, the message gets diluted.

That's where a manifesto comes in.

A manifesto is defined as "a published verbal declaration of the intentions, motives, or views of the issuer."[77] The most common types of manifestos are basic national documents like declarations of independence and constitutions.

---

77 Definition from Wikipedia.

One of the most enduring manifestos I've come across is the Johnson & Johnson credo. Created in 1943 by ex-Chairman Robert Wood Johnson, the credo maintains a hallowed place in J&J's culture to this day. It reads:

> *"We believe our first responsibility is to the doctors, nurses and patients, to mothers and fathers and all others **who use our products** and services. In meeting their needs everything we do must be of high quality. We must constantly strive to reduce our costs in order to maintain reasonable prices. Customers' orders must be serviced promptly and accurately. Our suppliers and distributors must have an opportunity to make a fair profit.*
>
> *We are responsible to our **employees**, the men and women who work with us throughout the world. Everyone must be considered as an individual. We must respect their dignity and recognize their merit. They must have a sense of security in their jobs. Compensation must be fair and adequate, and working conditions clean, orderly and safe. We must be mindful of ways to help our employees fulfill their family obligations. Employees must feel free to make suggestions and complaints. There must be equal opportunity for employment, development and advancement for those qualified. We must provide competent management, and their actions must be just and ethical.*
>
> *We are responsible to the **communities** in which we live and work and to the world community as well. We must be good citizens – support good works and charities and **pay our fair share of taxes**. We must encourage civic improvements and better health and education. We must maintain in good order the property we are privileged to use, **protecting the environment and natural resources**.*
>
> *Our final responsibility is to our **stockholders**. Business must make a sound profit. We must experiment with new ideas. Research must be carried on, innovative programs developed and mistakes paid for. New equipment must be purchased, new facilities provided and new products launched. Reserves must be created to provide for adverse times. When we operate according to these principles, the stockholders should realize a fair return."[78]*

In more recent times, we can see other very inspirational manifestos. Google's manifesto for example includes some great lines:

---

78 The original Johnson & Johnson credo can be viewed at www.jnj.com

> *"Focus on the user and all else will follow."*
> *"It's best to do one thing really, really well."*
> *"Fast is better than slow."*
> *"You can make money without doing evil."*[79]

And if you think about what Google does, generally speaking, most of us can agree nearly everything is couched around these founding ideas.

If you look at most company visions and missions, they tend to be a mishmash of idealistic statements of what they do and how big they would like to become. Generally, the company's mission and vision is something that is published on the website, put in the orientation of the company's new employees and then promptly forgotten. If you ask the majority of people about their company's vision and mission, you would get an answer that would amount to something akin to "we make great products and we try to make a lot of money." Of course, the company HR people would rather you believe there is a loftier mission but the reality of how it plays out in terms of pricing, service and HR policies invariably amounts to make products, be efficient and make money.

The other thing is that a company vision and mission are usually not longer than a sentence or two. This is partly to ensure that people can remember it all but also because it tries to mask the fact that the main goal of the company is really as a business entity and not much else.

A manifesto implies something that is rather different in the sense that everything the company does has to be part of a mission to meet the lofty standards of the manifesto. Every standard operating procedure, every product the company puts out (regardless of its income potential) and every company policy needs to be built around the manifesto.

The Price of Staying Silent

On the surface, the manifesto can be incredibly powerful for motivating internal employees. Yet for most of modern corporate history, companies have tended not to actively promote their manifestos or even create one in the first place. Instead, most companies would rather rely on splashy advertising campaigns that talk about what

---

79 You can read the full text of Google's "Ten Things We Know To Be True" at www.google.com/about/company/philosophy/

their products do or to provide some ideal picture of how you, as a customer, will be perfect only if you use their product.

It makes sense to hide behind an advertising campaign. In reality, ads are meant to psychologically affect us and to place an image in our mind that somehow we are just like the advertiser and their product. What could be more powerful, after all, than slogans like "I Want To Give The World a Coke" or "Where Do You Want to Go Today" (Microsoft's slogan for 20 years)? But this merely conceals the fact that the company is trying to sell you something as opposed to providing something of true value to society.

In fact, today much more so than ads from the mid-century, companies tend to couch their ad campaigns in catchy short phrases as opposed to direct statements of purpose. Even Apple's ads don't talk about "making a dent in the universe" anymore. The same goes for large companies like Pepsi, Ford, General Motors, Microsoft and GE. It's expensive enough to buy ad time. You would need a lot more than 30 seconds to describe your company's true meaning.

The idea of promoting a manifesto as the basis for the company is quite a new innovation as a result and rides on the back of all the things I've mentioned related to transparency brought about in the internet age. In a sense, companies that promote their manifesto in an active way are asking you to buy based on *why* they serve, not *what* they serve. And in fact, the internet was a major enabler for this in the sense that ad space and time is heavily restricted by cost whereas space on a webpage is technically limitless. In short, the internet gave you a place where you could air your entire manifesto at the same cost as a weak one-liner on your company's so-called vision and mission.

Setting It In Stone

The manifesto in itself is simply an articulation of everything that a company believes in. If you were asked to describe your entire value system, what you consider important and the person that you would like to be remembered as, you would be stating what in effect amounts to the personal equivalent of a manifesto. Each of us has deep ingrained desires for our own lives:

"I want to make money, and do so with dignity."

"I want to make a difference in the world through my activity with x social causes."

"I believe in treating people with kindness and generosity."

"I believe we should never lie, cheat or steal."

The Ultimate Journey

"I believe in always being honest and keeping my promises."

The manifesto is essentially the ultimate expression of humanizing our business interests. It is a clear, unequivocal statement of what you do, for whom you do it and what mark you want to leave on the world. It is NOT a marketing statement or a series of words on how you would like others to see you. It is NOT a general statement of being good at selling stuff. It is instead an unbreakable code of conduct, essentially the contract you agree to "sign" with each and every customer that you have. It is your story wrapped up in a few paragraphs or rules.

More than anything else though, and the main reason why many companies are still afraid to actually write one, the manifesto is a clear statement of with who you will *and won't* do business. It effectively limits your customers to those who believe in the exact same things as you and discourages or entirely excludes people who are not looking for the same thing. This last point is the scariest aspect for most marketers and companies in that it basically gives you a line at which you carve away a substantial portion of the potential market out there. In many cases, your manifesto could exclude as much as 99% of the population in one fell swoop.

That said, this is no reason to freak out. If you think about how much money companies spend marketing to the wrong kind of people, it is a pretty substantial drain on the budget with no outcome. This has always been "the elephant in the room" for many marketers; on the one hand, marketers are asked to spend money on channels that approximately reflect their targeted demographics, yet at the same time, not everyone in that demographic is necessarily suited to their products or brand.

Designing Your Manifesto

Step 1: Start at the Beginning

The process of coming up with what should be in your manifesto can vary depending on the age of your company or brand and how consistent your company has been in the past. Manifestos are generally ideal for companies that boast a strong culture or are aspiring to that end. Generally, a company is founded for a few basic purposes, of which making heaps of money is only one reason. Usually, companies are started by people with a specific passion for a business or a goal to serve a basic need of society that is not yet being met.

So for a company, the starting point of the manifesto is to go back to the beginning and discover why the company was created and what was the character of its founders. For example, you could look at Apple founders Steve Jobs and Steve Wozniak and look at how they wanted to bring a computer to everyone and to empower the individual to be as strong as the company. You could look at Howard Schultz of Starbucks and see how he desired to bring the feel and culture of the Italian sidewalk café experience to America and create a meeting point. Invariably, almost every great business starts with a high level of passion for something rather than an unbridled effort to just make a lot of money.

Step 2: Identify Who Your Ideal Customers AND Employees Should Be

When I took a course from the Disney Institute on how to achieve business excellence, one of the first lessons they teach is that you cannot achieve anything with customers without first having a great team. If your employees are not aligned with what the product and company is supposed to do, things tend to fall flat.

If you can define the basic characteristics of what kind of people you would want to hire, that solves a major part of your manifesto since in essence, your customer should align perfectly with the people who work in your organization. For example, Disney focuses on enriching experiences for families and children. Their employees and their manifesto revolve around qualities to foster that. A music festival organizer's team might have a specific love of music and bringing people together, meaning the company's products and manifesto would follow from there. If a person didn't correspond to your company's basic principles you would neither hire nor sell to them. In this way, the manifesto is already starting to limit down your community.

Step 3: Define the Ideal World for Your Team and Customers

One thing to understand is that even after you have a manifesto, you will never "go from 0-60" in a few seconds. A true manifesto is an expression of what you are committed to achieve. You'll acknowledge that at the time of writing the manifesto you are not yet perfect but that you are on a journey to take everyone to that perfect place. You might never reach it or you might make mistakes along the way, but the manifesto lays out the path for you. The manifesto is in a way a statement of where you would *like* to go, not where you already are.

Step 4: Use Action Words that Mean Something

The call to action is one of the most crucial parts of the manifesto. Any company willing to write a manifesto is automatically drawing a line in the sand that they will not appeal to everyone, and that's ok. Strong verbs help you to articulate that call to action.

- "Will" or "Do" (strong verbs) vs. "Want" or "Try" (weak verbs)
- "Believe" (strong) vs. "Hope" (weak)
- "Make" (strong) vs. "Find" (weak)
- "Follow" (strong) vs. "Search" (weak)
- "Do Not" (strong) vs. "Avoid" (weak)

When I say strong verbs, we are talking not as if we are delegating responsibility or asking nicely. Use the kinds of words you might use when you are literally shaking sense into someone. The manifesto is no place for being timid. This is about certainty – what you believe and would do and what you absolutely, positively don't and would never believe.

One last point that I can't emphasize enough is to avoid clichés at all costs. I talked earlier about "Fixed Stare" syndrome and the idea that anyone who has been around the marketing profession long enough invariably slips into a haze where their copywriting descends into clichés that they've seen a thousand other people use. There are no templates for manifestos. Each manifesto should be 100% different from any other. You cannot simply lift words from other companies. Similarly, using vague generic terms like "Simply the Best" or "We're With You Wherever You Go" will leave your manifesto vague and confusing.[80]

The result of going through these four steps is your manifesto. This all seems rather theoretical, so perhaps this is a good time to tell you a couple of stories, one is my own, the other of a very good friend of mine.

The Fashion Beliefs and How They Came to Be

I have managed the fashion brands division for Time International, an Indonesian retailer, for close to a decade now. Over the first seven years, we had actually been extremely successful. Growth of the business during that time was more than eightfold from our early years. In spite of the financial crisis that hit in 2008-2010, we had actually held up quite well with a net double-digit growth during those years.

---

80 An entire website was created to map out some of the worst marketing clichés ever. You can check them out at 101cliches.com. My best advice is to avoid using any of those slogans in your manifesto (or in any of your marketing material for that matter).

We had been operating a watch-only concept called WatchTime International since 2005, a multi-brand watch and handbag chain called Urban Icon since 2009 and had operated the brand stores for Fossil since 2008. With the world coming out of recession (in starts and stops) and with the Indonesian economy picking up steam and being mentioned in the same breath as other emerging economies like South Africa, Turkey and even India, everything seemed on the rise.

However, there was an enduring sense among most of us that we had failed to tell the story, internally or externally, about the great things that we were doing. In earlier days, the success or failure of our team was still primarily defined by how much revenue and profit we made. As our business grew, we technically cared for our customers and teammates but it was very much in a transactional, "You pay me, I give you good products" kind of way. For those who worked in the business for a long time, there was nothing to really rally behind.

At the end of 2010, I was introduced to a speech given by Simon Sinek during a TEDx event and to his concept of "The Golden Circle" as a means of explaining your business to the outside world.[81] I started to read more about purpose-based management and, as a storyteller, I wondered whether there was a way that we could articulate what we do in a more concise manner.

At the beginning of 2011, armed with the input of my team, I sat for barely three hours and constructed what became known as the Fashion Beliefs. It's easy to think that the manifesto is a long, complicated document that needs the participation of many people to write. The truth is that manifestos are usually the fastest and easiest documents to write. Speaking as a writer, I also knew the business intricately, I knew the impact of our products, and was under no illusion that since our products were not a basic physical human necessity there had to be a much deeper meaning why people bought them. Through years of experience, I knew the exact reason why major parts of our business had been put in place – the people we hired, the prices we set, the products we chose. So for us, the manifesto was actually already in our head. It was just waiting to come out. It just so happened that I was tasked with putting it to paper.

Because the manifesto was also an expression of what we collectively *felt*, I found it easier to write the first draft on my own. Everyone says that brainstorming is supposed to be better for creativity. I never felt that to be true. When you brainstorm, you tend to compromise on basic principles. As well, since most people are

---

81   As mentioned earlier, the concept of The Golden Circle is well explained in Simon Sinek's 2009 book "Start with Why: How Great Leaders Inspire Everyone". The book is pretty much a must-read for anyone interested in the basic concept of purpose-based management.

not attuned to openly sharing their feelings and putting themselves "into a corner" with those feelings, doing the manifesto for me could only be something that was written by the key "vision" person of the department. It's not always the CEO or President, but most generally they have the widest idea of the limits of the business' behavior and since they need to buy into it 100%, the first draft was not something that could be allocated to a group.

I started with a basic foundation for the manifesto – a background of sorts. The first step was to empathize with the human need that enabled us to exist. In doing so, it was important to imagine the kinds of challenges, aspirations and pressures facing people who visited us every day.

The Story of Our Business

Each day, our customers and employees have the hardest of lives. They work hard, try to eke out a living in an increasingly competitive world and suffer from the stress of asking themselves, "Am I good enough?", "Am I rich enough?", "Am I beautiful enough?", "Am I successful enough?", "Do people like me?", "Am I special?"

And yet, everywhere they go, they are bombarded with messages offering to answer all of these questions if only they pay some money or work harder. Yet people who sell them these things or make them work harder aren't interested in solving their problems; they're interested in solving their own, even if it's not what their customer or employee really needs.

The end result? They are more stressed and unsure of whether they are doing the right thing. They float around this life in a state of uncertainty, never quite sure if what they are doing is right, if they are following the right advice (and advisors) and more importantly, if they are accepted by others for who they are.

So in this case, we defined the problem, touched on empathizing with them as human beings and basically defined our reason for being.

The next part involved defining what kind of people we desired to be. Basic words that came to mind were drawn from how we operated as a company and from those stresses. Most of all we wanted to focus on the ideas that:

- We are a little non-conformist, we like "different" stuff. The strength of our brands was that each had a different story and was not really like the common products that were found in the market.
- Honesty is a fundamental human value for our team.

- Being in a service business, we wanted to provide a terrific experience to make people feel as good as possible – this is what we wanted for ourselves when we went shopping.
- We wanted our team to "reach for the brass ring", not just settling at being ok. We assumed that each of our team members had the chance to achieve greatness in their respective jobs. Initially, we thought greatness was just about achieving great financial results but over time, we gradually all realized that since we couldn't pay the highest salaries, at least we could try to help our team reach a level of personal achievement and improvement that would make them the best they could be.

So now it was time to take the problem and talk about our fundamental reason for existing.

Why We're Here

- *We believe that it is our job in the midst of all this stress to give our customers and employees a little peace of mind.*
- *We believe no matter who you are or where you are, you have the RIGHT to look as good as you can, to feel as special, accepted and loved as possible and to be an inspiration to others.*
- *We believe in being honest to everyone we meet (customer and employee), to treat them with dignity, seeing them as people, rather than as dollar signs.*
- *We believe that each of us has a little bit of greatness inside of us. It's not enough to just be the same or even just good as others. If we help each other out, we'll all fulfill our potential as part of our community and mankind.*
- *We believe being special is way more fulfilling than just being like everyone else.*

So here we've achieved in wrapping up the basic aspects of what we offer to the world. Notice that we've actively attempted to exclude people who just want a product and called to action people who believe that what we do is part of something greater that's worth caring about. Notice also that the language being used was very direct and unequivocal.

"We Believe"

It was us saying, "Let there be no doubt". We did not include words such as "hope", "aspire", "trying" or "want". Those kinds of words imply that we're on a short expedition that we might or might not continue to pursue. In other words, your destination could be one of many. When you *believe* in something, there is no going back. You have one goal, one destination. It's like "greatness or bust" in a way.

The difference between "We Believe" and "We Are" is also a bit nuanced. "We Are" would have been a good wording if we had been pursuing this mission for a long time and were in the midst of achieving it. "We Believe" allowed us to say that we're still a "work in progress" but that we will do everything possible to get there.

But since the "why we're here" aspect contains a few points, we felt it would be great to wrap it up in one nice package that would *drive* people to action.

> *Everyone else believes in just getting by. We believe in the greatness of every individual. By helping others to achieve this greatness, we ourselves achieve our potential as human beings. We can all be special.*
> *Our Mission: "To Make Special People Look and Feel Amazing!!"*

Actually, the last line should go on top, but I've written it at the bottom because it was actually the last thing I thought of when I wrote it. It was a "1 + 1 + 1 equals AMAZING!!!" kind of thing.

When the Beliefs were presented to my team, the draft was adopted without a single change. It encapsulated everything that everyone knew to be true. When presented it to the shareholders, it was passed within five minutes.

Within weeks, we started to act on it, changing office procedures, store operating procedures, how we evaluated our people and even who we kept and didn't keep.

The interesting thing about our manifesto was that while we were really proud of it internally, the fact that we had not always been perfect in fulfilling it made us apprehensive to promote it externally. Nevertheless, during that time our income nearly tripled. This shows how manifestos can be incredibly powerful even just as an internal marketing tool.

But to find out about someone who externalized it and what it meant, I would like to introduce you to Edward Suhadi.

More Than Just a Photo Album

The first time you meet Edward you get the sense of a gentle giant. A somewhat heavyset six-foot-plus ball of unbridled creativity, Edward is a person who exudes humility. He speaks in a slow, measured tone, always evaluating his next words before speaking them. Lost in the midst of an industry where $100,000 weddings are more the norm than the exception, it's interesting to discover how down-to-earth Edward really is.

An avowed fan of advertising since his early years, Edward grew up aspiring to be a creative director in an ad agency before the world of photography called on him to establish his own studio in 2004. When he started his business, he founded it on the hallmark of honesty.

"Since I was a kid, I loved advertising. So after a while I got into photography. I always wanted to be a creative director for an agency," says Edward. "I learned that my passion was storytelling. How can I tell a story with pictures, video and writing?"

And that storytelling was just what he did for about seven years. Gradually the business grew as he and his studio became better known and busier, especially as Indonesia's economy continued to grow and the middle class yearned for more and more exotic shows of wealth in their wedding events. Edward found himself being invited around the world to take pre-wedding and wedding photos.

But after a while, something was awakened in him. "I was never good at dealing with egomaniacs. I felt after a while in our business, we had a lot of 'Princess Brides', people who had huge egos. When people want to feed their egos, they want to pump up the glitz and the fireworks. 2011 was the best year for business; we got to do weddings and pre-weddings internationally. But we were working on autopilot. It seemed there were too many client complaints, not because we did a bad job but because we didn't do the job they wanted us to do."

So in the latter part of 2011, Edward decided to do something about it. He essentially changed his way of doing business, shunning clients who wanted to do photo shoots outside the country simply for the purpose of one-upping their friends or allowing multiple changes in the albums. In essence, he decided to stop taking the standard wedding photos that he viewed as being clichéd and inauthentic and decided to start shooting weddings as a true story, one in which there were no scripts and where every wedding was unique based on the individual character of the couple.

In doing so, he started turning away clients, a lot of them. Profit dropped by more than 85% in a year as he jettisoned his Princess Bride clients for others who understood the art behind the storytelling.

But before doing so, he prefaced it with a story about where he was going to take the business. In November 2011, Edward wrote a blog entry entitled "A Promise of a Revolution" to explain his new philosophy, his manifesto.

"I am dying inside. A slow painful death. It is because things have become too rigid, too predictable. Too many terms and conditions, too many preset expectations.

It's a funny thing happening these days: Clients hire a creative person/entity to do creative work, but the end result is already set in their mind. Coming into a meeting with all the references from magazines and blogs, they know that they want to be shot like this, wearing this dress, on that location. And we, the creative persons, agree to this. Out of ignorance, out of our mediocrity, and out of our need for the business.

I know the industry will not change overnight, and I know Edward Suhadi Productions cannot change overnight either. But as the captain of this ship, I will promise you this:

We will change bit by bit, eliminating destructive dogmas and habits, and adding creativity and freedom to our work. We will shoot more of what we love for the clients that trust us. We will not ask, "How would you like to be shot?", but "This is how we are going to shoot you." We will try never try things and dictate on how things are going to be done from now on. Sounds arrogant, but believe me, it is the only way to give space and freedom for creativity and great work to soar.

We know that this might put is in the corner, and this will lose us some business, and some people are gonna' hate us. But at least we go home knowing that we have done something wonderful to a few. We are definitely not going to be the best, but at least we 'really' tried to be."[82]

And from then on, Edward started writing about the art of his industry and calling on his colleagues to return to their roots. He wrote a full manifesto which he named "Pictures to Remember" that served as an emotional call to his clients to remind them why wedding pictures existed.

Power to the People

"A Promise of a Revolution" is a very straight, unedited, unpolished description of what Edward feels. In previous decades, it would be almost unthinkable to write in this style. Surely, it would be considered "too rough", "too honest". Whereas in the 80s and 90s, marketers wanted to (and were largely successful) in defining how

---

82 "A Promise of a Revolution" by Edward Suhadi (2011). The full text can be viewed at blog.edwardsuhadi.com/2011/11/27/a-promise-of-a-revolution/

people viewed their products through their communications, Edward recognized that in the ultra-connected "We-World" of the 21st century, people are looking to relate to the companies they support. As he so rightly points out "When I write, I always imagine people nodding their heads."

This last quote is the ultimate expression of a great manifesto or powerful copywriting. Knowing that 21st century citizens have become deeply cynical of the marketing messages that are thrown at them on almost a per-second basis, it would be fair to assume that people are anxious to hear someone (anyone) who will "give it to them straight". The fact that the choices in any given product are so aplenty only adds to that anxiety as people search, re-search and re-re-search to affirm that they have made the right choice on their purchase. Anyone who has tried booking a hotel online recently is surely a case in point of this.

So what kind of writing tips can we take away from our study of manifestos?

Lesson 1: Write the Story BEFORE You Write the Manifesto

One aspect of the manifesto that you can see in the two examples above is that actually there's usually a "story before the story". In other words, the manifesto doesn't come out of nowhere. So while a lot of people do get to see the final manifesto (i.e.: the To Do's), they rarely get to see the story of what prompted the writer to think that something was inherently wrong with the world.

The preface to a manifesto is really important because your manifesto actually exists *because* of it. And in fact, because the existing condition is so incredibly wrong/offensive/crazy, a company or its founder may be "fired up" to create or work toward a "better world".

In my view, it's really hard to write a great manifesto without writing the preface. In writing the preface, you actually get yourself psychologically more ready to write a great manifesto.

Lesson 2: Use the "So What?" Test

Earlier on, we talked about the use of the "So What?" process to evolve your thinking to get to the big picture of your business. The manifesto is the perfect exercise for you to utilize "So What?". The one thing about the manifesto is that it must be resolute and meaningful to all your employees and all your customers. The "So What?" test allows you to evaluate whether your story has gone far enough.

Lesson 3: Say it Like You Mean it

When you write, do it with purpose. Use action words that imply absolutes, not wishful thinking.

Lesson 4: Make it Yours

Avoid the use of clichés. Think about what you are saying and strive for 100% clarity. If after you write the manifesto, it looks as if no other company or brand in the world could have applied the same thing, it means you did a great job. Remember that a manifesto is a statement of beliefs; it's not a marketing tool. Yet because of the fact that it is so purpose-oriented, it's probably the ultimate expression that you can make of your story.

Lesson 5: Integrate It Into Your Story

Once you have a manifesto, it needs to be integrated into a central part of your ongoing story. Each product and each message you put out goes back to the manifesto. If we look at the process of journey-writing, we talk about the first stage, The Idea. A company would only go ahead to make a product if it matched its reason for being. It just so happens the latter is already conveniently found in your manifesto.

Similarly, the manifesto can serve as a starting point to all your upcoming content. If we look at how Edward Suhadi managed his marketing, an entire line of storytelling from his blog was founded on the tone and content of his manifesto. If your company is about promoting better health, that's what should be in your blogs and your product promotions should touch back on the founding principles of a larger mission. If your organization is about creating a new generation of leaders, that's what your blogs and product descriptions will emphasize.

If you want to talk about powerful storytelling, the manifesto is kind of the granddaddy of them all. How you present it is up to you. You can use fancy typography, cute diagrams or just words on paper depending on your organization's orientation and capability. If you view the manifesto as an unbreakable code of conduct for you, your team, your products and your customers, it serves as the foundation for every word you will ever write to follow it.

In truth, most businesses have a manifesto in their heads but just never articulate it. Most companies do fine without a manifesto. Globally, the level of workers who are "engaged" in their jobs hovers somewhere between 30-60% depending on which study you read.[83] Whatever is the true number, if you combined the high number of disengaged workers and the earlier figures we noted in which at least half of global consumers don't trust companies in general, there is a tremendous amount of value in trust-building. The manifesto and how you keep to it is the ultimate trust-building exercise.

---

83   This data is taken from two sources, Gallup's "2013 State of the American Workplace" survey which covered 150,000 workers and Aon Hewitt's "Trends in Global Employee Engagement 2013" which covered 2,500 companies representing 3.8 million employees.

SIXTEEN

ARE THE PATIENTS RUNNING THE ASYLUM?

Going Beyond the Press Release

WIZARD: Why, anybody can have a brain. That's a very mediocre commodity. Every pusillanimous creature that crawls on the earth or slinks through slimy seas has a brain! From the rock-bound coast of Maine to the Sun ... oh - oh, no - ah - Well, be that as it may. Back where I come from we have universities, seats of great learning where men go to become great thinkers. And when they come out, they think deep thoughts and with no more brains than you have ... But! They have one thing you haven't got! A diploma! Therefore, by virtue of the authority vested in me by the Universitatus Committeeatum e pluribis unum, I hereby confer upon you the honorary degree of Th.D.

SCARECROW: Th.D.?

WIZARD: Yeah – that ... that's Dr. of Thinkology!

- The Wizard of Oz (1939)[84]

---

84   The Wizard of Oz. Dir. Victor Fleming. Metro-Goldwyn-Mayer, 1939.

In my life, I've run the gamut from journalist to catalogue hack to storyteller. In that time, one of the biggest problems that I see in people who try to sell a product is that they (falsely) assume that everyone cares about their brand. I talked in Chapter 4 about the fallacy of the 98% Rule. Recall that I explained how you would be most correct in assuming 98% of the world *doesn't* care or know about your product or brand. Even among the remaining 2% who do know you, only a small percentage of those people will generally have a favorable opinion of you.

The absolute same reality exists when it comes to the media. In the past, our sole form of storytelling came through press coverage. We would send press releases to as many media outlets as possible and invested our time in trying to get them to know us, perhaps through visiting their office or inviting them to lunch, holding press events or using an agency which had a relationship with these editors or reporters.

In today's business world, our options are no longer limited to merely satisfying the press. If we talk about the manifesto as our starting point to telling our story internally and our approach to apologizing publicly to our customers as an ongoing loop in the cycle (see Chapter 17), we need to look at some of the other avenues that are available to us to perpetuate our story. If you are an experienced marketer, many of these will seem obvious. For those who are newer to the field, there are a few channels that you might not have considered.

The Year of Living Vicariously

If you read classical press releases, most are written to *tell* journalists what to write. These press releases usually come in a glossy packet containing some nice photos and a full functional breakdown of all the benefits and features of the product.

In every respect, this is to be expected. The first lesson taught in journalism school is the 5 Ws. For many marketers, the press release is the only story they know how to tell, so by default they tend to go back to the old standbys and focus on feature, function and glossy photos (the 3 Fs).

Sometimes, the old glossy press pack or fax does work with less demanding media. My former editor at University of Western Ontario's "The Gazette", Eliotte Friedman, who currently serves as an anchor on the long-running show "Hockey Night in Canada", once told me the difference between our campus newspaper and the local daily, was that we actually went out and chased stories while they just copied word-for-word the press releases they received. Occasionally, you do find people who will print your story without asking questions.

However, more often than not, the media types who can really impact people are much more demanding. Those who work for themselves (think bloggers) want content that is exclusive and geared toward their niche. Those who work for publications want content that has more punch or perhaps can even help pay their bills.

The key point is that the story should come first with the function occupying more of a footnote. Instead, think about these techniques:

- Make sure you have established your brand's story before you start pushing individual products. If you are using an agency, they will usually try to arrange some kind of meeting with your targeted reporters in the early stages of your engagement. This is a perfect time to tell the story of your journey in person.
- Once your journey is established, be sure to use "ST" words as a bedrock for your argument to win the press over.
- Speak in a tone that seeks to share as opposed to dictating what will be written.
- Help people to live vicariously through you.

In my experience, that last point is particularly potent. Let me give some examples.

When I started Backpack Asia, a tourism public relations startup, we had no money for advertising and were hopelessly undercapitalized from the outset. Despite those obstacles, our launch event was covered in newspapers in three countries.

Our company's main mission was to promote the idea of backpack travel as an alternative to traditional tours or luxury travel. Our story was rooted largely from my experiences as a backpacker years earlier. Our press gatherings and all of our releases focused heavily on the nostalgia of backpacking. We talked about our experiences, featured photos of some of the sites that traditional tourists might never come across. And we talked about how the backpack movement was bigger than a lot of media had ever imagined, meaning that it was something that many people could easily attain.

A lot of people (media included) idealized the prospect of backpacking but most wouldn't actually "be able" to do it. As such, we provided a way for people to connect to the hobby vicariously through us. The connection was sufficiently compelling that we received a level of coverage that might ordinarily never be given to such a small company.

Sometimes, the law of living vicariously need not take a written form. If your journey or story is strong enough, the right people just hear about it organically.

Take the case of TOMS. Blake Mycoskie likes to tell the story of how he was contacted by Vogue Editor-in-Chief Anna Wintour completely out of the blue based on what she had heard about the brand. Wintour liked the shoes but *loved* the attachment to TOMS' mission. She intuitively understood how exposing the TOMS journey would enable her readers to live vicariously through the company's mission and to feel good about looking good, even if they never actually saw a disadvantaged child receive a new pair of shoes. TOMS was featured in Vogue and the free publicity led to them winning several major accounts.

So in truth, storytelling is deeply rooted in press relations in general. Sometimes you need to write the story using the concepts of a journey, the right tone and establishing the urgency through "ST" words. Other times, opinion leaders are just drawn to your journey and you don't even need to tap a single key to get press coverage.

The Audacity of Books

There are lots of leaders who are truly fantastic storytellers for their brand and this enables them to get out the whole story without relying on the press to interpret it for them. We can even draw a parallel to the political world. Take for example how Barack Obama's campaign for the presidency started in earnest with the success of his book "The Audacity of Hope" which went beyond the stump speeches and political ads to deliver a compelling story about his life and beliefs and set the stage for a mass mobilization of enthusiastic volunteers.

A lot of other great leaders have gone out and written books that expanded on their life experiences and thus made the brand larger than before, sometimes even during the relatively early stages of their company. I would point to leaders like Tony Hsieh of Zappos, Blake Mycoskie of TOMS, Lee Iacocca of Chrysler and Howard Schultz of Starbucks as just a few leaders who have used books to raise awareness about their brands, their missions and their journeys.

Because of the technical difficulty of writing a book, this is a somewhat lesser-used method of storytelling. However, the prevailing notion that many have is that anyone who publishes a book must generally know what they're talking about, added to the fact that most of the books written about brands relate to companies that are reasonably well-known, means these books tend to be accepted by readers without reservation. A book is about sharing knowledge and there is a tremendous amount of goodwill that can be gained with such a noble purpose.

The Ultimate Journey

There are a lot of more experienced authors than me, so I won't present myself as the ultimate authority on the subject. However, based on my observation, following the tenets of transparency, relatability and most importantly focusing your book on sharing lessons that others can apply in self-promotion are keys to successfully evolving your story. Never forget, people read books so they can be entertained and learn. In another words, great books entail the very essence of great storytelling.

All About Us

It's no accident that the trend toward storytelling started to kick into high gear with the evolution of the internet. The ability to publish an unlimited amount of information at no additional cost was a huge step forward from when stories had to be kept as short as possible or even skipped altogether due to the financial cost associated with excessive words.

Most people view their company's website as a place to push their product and don't even think to push their stories. This is a huge mistake. In fact, while the About Us section is rarely the most promoted or viewed page on a company's website, it also has huge potential as a reference point to all your stories.

In fact, many of the best companies use the tenets of journey storytelling as the foundation of their About Us (or Our Story) section. This can be incredibly powerful. Holstee.com is a great example of using their journey to set up a greater engagement with the company. Thebodyshop.com does a tremendous job of talking about their developing journey and awesome events on a highly visible part of their home page. Shinola, a company dedicated to recreating the story of industrial revival in Detroit does an extensive discussion of their journey at shinola.com. At TOMS.com, their journey and their many awesome events are covered in their "Stories and Videos" and "One for One" sections.

The obvious question to ask is what if your company does not have some kind of altruistic mission. Well, my simple answer is that Holstee sells t-shirts, The Body Shop sells skincare products, Shinola sells watches and accessories and TOMS sells shoes. None of these products are particularly inspiring on their own. The very fact that these companies have invested so much time and effort in exposing their journey and telling an ongoing story, and the success that all have found in one way or another, just goes to show how powerful storytelling can be. Most of these companies actually started their business on the internet, so it wasn't as if they had years of scale to go by. The point is, any company can use their website to tell a story that can be seen by customers, friends, partners and media 24/7.

I'm not saying that your story needs to overshadow your products and selling functions on your website. I'm merely suggesting that it should share the headlines and be easily found, and that once users click into it, the section should show a considerable effort to incorporate the various lessons I've spoken about throughout this book.

The Blog

A lot of companies have started blogs as a means of expanding their story. The benefits of writing content that is focused around your story (as opposed to selling) are fairly obvious. The most distinctive point that I would like to make is to not focus on writing a blog just to have one but rather with an aim to be curator-worthy

Curation on large sites and even by individuals is becoming a massive trend. On content agglomerating apps like Flipboard and Zite, anyone can curate their own e-magazines and share them with others. Our Twitter accounts, our Pinterest boards and our Instagram photos and videos are all examples of how we curate content. In previous days, we might have expressed our inner diva by singing in the shower. In the 21st century, we exercise our inner publisher in a lot of new ways.

We talked earlier about Ronnie Singh and his experience at 2K Sports. Ronnie's ability to weave his encounters with athletes playing the game, his own personal view of the progress of the game, his experience playing the game and other things he likes has become an integral sub-plot in the success of the 2K story, particularly the NBA2K franchise. While 2K does issue press releases, Ronnie's tweets and even his live videos provide a more trusted source for just about everyone.

Or look at Edward Suhadi and his "A Promise of a Revolution" blog post. Instead of putting out press releases, he stated his story in words that the average person could understand through a blog on his website. The message spread among his enthusiastic clients who curated through retweets and telling the story to their friends and by him enlisting influential people who were attracted by the prospect of being a part of his continuing story.

Invariably, your one and only question when writing a brand blog should not be "do I like my blog?" but rather "do I think that people will share/curate this story?"

Some great blogging tips:

- If you notice the chapter and section titles that I've used in this book, these are generally short and catchy. These are perfect to be re-tweeted by readers.
- Keep your story focused. Make sure the blog has one specific angle that is attached to your journey and stick to it. In that way, you can become a trusted expert in one topic.
- Write in the first-person. This ensures that you stay personable instead of seeming too commercial.
- Express your passion via "ST" words. These create urgency and trust.

In the end, all of these various types of content can leave a lasting footprint from your story that is accessible for all. Thankfully we have so many more options than just a couple of decades ago, so it's important to not just focus on one type.

Clearly, none of this is new to experienced marketers. But as I mentioned previously, the goal of this book is to get you to think holistically about your storytelling, not merely as a way to sell or as a byproduct of your product. The story needs to stay front and center in all of your marketing efforts. Blogs, books, About Us sections and even press releases (not to mention videos, advertisements, packaging and a myriad of other non-written channels that are available) are ways for you to publicize your journey and to promote your ongoing story so that you can amplify your message to customers with each new product release. The lessons we spoke about earlier, expressing passion and empathy, using tense and tone to articulate your voice and use of superlatives to establish why people should listen to you, are all elements that don't end once your company has already released a few seasons or even years of products.

In a sense this hearkens us back to our earlier significantobjects.com story. The choice to be seen as a $2 mini-bottle of mayonnaise or a $51 collector's item really depends on whether you view storytelling as a one-off anomaly or a constant "lifeblood of the brand" task in every part of your communications strategy.

SEVENTEEN

A THOUSAND WAYS TO SAY YOU'RE SORRY

The Art of the Apology

JERRY: This used to be my specialty. I was good in a living room. Send me in there; I'll do it alone. And now I just... I don't know... but on what was supposed to be the happiest night of my business life, it wasn't complete, wasn't nearly close to being in the same vicinity as complete, because I couldn't share it with you. I couldn't hear your voice, or laugh about it with you. I missed my wife. We live in a cynical world, and we work in a business of tough competitors, so try not to laugh – I love you. You complete me.

- Jerry Maguire (1996)[85]

---

85 Jerry Maguire. Dir. Cameron Crowe. TriStar Pictures, 1996.

I started my first company when I was barely 25 years old and still extremely naïve. For a person who loved their product like I did (which was tourism PR), it was shocking how little I knew about such "mundane" things as human resources and legal affairs. I mean, you could be a Tony Hsieh of Zappos and start a fashion company thanks to a greater knowledge in people management rather than fashion. Some people are just naturally skilled at the art of people management. I, unfortunately, was not one of those people.

I did have help ... sort of. A brother of a close friend of mine offered to help me navigate the somewhat archaic code of the Malaysian labor law. Somewhere in the course of that document, there is a regulation stating that you have to give employees a minimum of 10 national holidays (out of about 20 that are actually on the calendar). My HR consultant suggested that I give the team their option of days off. Looking back, it was probably the most misguided advice anyone has ever given me.

Hours later, my most senior teammate and marketing manager, Darren, put his resignation letter on my desk. He was a guy I trusted without question. For all my inexperienced enthusiasm as an entrepreneur, Darren was the guy who would tell me when my ideas were terrible and gave me the pulse of how everyone on my team was thinking. When he explained the issue, I immediately knew what was wrong and asked him to hold onto it for a day.

Within a couple of hours, I had sent an email apologizing to everyone and posted on the wall the full calendar of national holidays for everyone.

Darren took back his resignation letter. The rest of the team decided to stick around too.

I'm not trumpeting myself as a hero of virtue. Quite the opposite, I'm not ashamed to admit that I've done my share of stupid things in business and in life, and this was one of the bigger ones. The point here is that whether you're in a small company or you're a big brand, as humans, we're bound to mess up, either with an individual customer or with an entire product line or corporate action.

The Power of Saying Sorry

It goes without saying that in the litigation-heavy environment of a country like the US, it's not always easy to make an apology. On certain critical actions, apologizing in a totally transparent way can get you into serious legal hot soup. Imagine a doctor saying to a family after a relative dies on an operating table: "Umm, during the operation, I kinda … uh, made a wrong cut. Now your relative is dead. Oops … I'm really sorry." That could conceivably be a multi-million dollar admission. So theoretically you can't just apologize without regard for the consequences.

My brother-in-law, an orthopedic surgeon, once told me a little-known fact (well, for those of us outside the medical profession anyway). It seems most malpractice cases actually arise because the doctor was not forthright with the patient and their family before the incident about the potential negative outcomes. By glossing over the possible complications of any treatment in the effort to give "hope", any bad outcome results in a sense of distrust and betrayal that often drives already distraught people to lash out at anyone they can … and sue them for a LOT of money.

There's no doubt that in the age of the 24-hour social media cycle, we are part of an ongoing conversation with our friends, guests, customers and employees. That ongoing conversation represents a journey and story of a different kind that is being constantly updated. We spend a lot of time building up trust through various types of marketing, including the kind of storytelling I've discussed up to now. Still, one incident can drive that all down the tubes. That said, how you recover from the issue can say more about you and your company than the mistake ever did.

Take two very contrary cases to show just how different responses can be.

In July 2013, Asiana Airlines Flight 214 rammed into a seawall upon descent to San Francisco International Airport, killing three Chinese citizens. Days later, the company published the following apology:

"We at Asiana Airlines would like to express our utmost sympathy and regret to the passengers of OZ flight 214 and their families as a result of this accident. We apologize most deeply."

That doesn't feel like a deep apology …

Now let's look at Apple. Seen as a company that could do no wrong, in 2012, it released iOS 6, complete with Apple Maps, meant to "make a dent in the universe" (and in Google Maps). Instead, the maps were horribly inaccurate, sometimes leading to roads that didn't exist, other times even instructing drivers to drive over cliffs in order to get to their destination.

A year prior, when the iPhone 4 came out and industry magazines pointed to weakened signal strength when holding the phone in certain ways, the late Steve Jobs had a simple method of "apology":

"Just avoid holding it that way."[86]

Straight, to the point, no BS. It's your fault, stop being a dumbass. Strangely, people who idolized Apple and Jobs seemed to be ok with that response. I guess some people can do no wrong.

A year after Jobs' premature passing, new CEO Tim Cook responded somewhat differently to the Apple Maps situation.

> *"At Apple, we strive to make world-class products that deliver the best experience possible to our customers. With the launch of our new Maps last week, we fell short on this commitment. We are extremely sorry for the frustration this has caused our customers and we are doing everything we can to make Maps better.*
>
> *While we're improving Maps, you can try alternatives by downloading map apps from the App Store like Bing, MapQuest and Waze, or use Google or Nokia maps by going to their websites and creating an icon on your home screen to their web app.*
>
> *Everything we do at Apple is aimed at making our products the best in the world. We know that you expect that from us, and we will keep working non-stop until Maps lives up to the same incredibly high standard.*
>
> *Tim Cook*
> *Apple's CEO"*[87]

Quite a change in tone. It just goes to show you that even the companies that are most admired sometimes need to eat humble pie. In Apple's case, the failure of Apple Maps didn't dampen enthusiasm for upcoming releases of hardware or software. The Apple Maps debacle was just a bump in the road of a longer story of Apple making huge dents in the universe. Failures like Apple Maps over time actually become a positive part of the story. In turns out that sometimes, companies are like people; they can actually look more heroic because they tripped and fell along the way.

Of course, some people never learn. Take this reply by Ryanair's Michael O'Leary to a customer who paid a rather exorbitant amount to print off her ticket at the airport.

"We think Mrs. McLeod should pay 60 euros for being so stupid," he said. *"She wasn't able to print her boarding card because, as you know, there are no internet cafes in*

---

86 Steve Jobs, from customer email, June 24, 2010.
87 Apology letter from Apple, September 2012.

The Ultimate Journey

Alicante, no hotels where they could print them out for you, and you couldn't get to a fax machine so some friend at home can print them and fax them to you. She wrote to me last week asking for compensation and a gesture of goodwill. To which we have replied, politely but firmly, thank you Mrs. McLeod but it was your ****-up."[88]

... And all this in exchange for buying a cheap ticket.

In a twisted postscript to the whole situation, O'Leary even admitted months later that perhaps Ryanair had gone too far and might reconsider its many efforts to annoy people. For better or worse, Ryanair's story got stuck at "fly cheap".[89] Ryanair is still extremely successful, but only insofar as they can keep prices low and are bigger than the other guys. Keep in mind though, that's a pretty expensive story to maintain. I doubt most brands would like to be seen in the way that Ryanair is viewed.

Companies have been apologizing for as long as there have been companies. Whether it is through full-page advertisements, appearances on shows like "60 Minutes" or direct visits to affected victims, the apology has become as much a part of marketing as after-sales service.

A 2010 poll taken by Harris Interactive showed that in a survey of 2,151 adults, more than 50% distrusted companies in all industries. Banks had a confidence rating of just 20%, down by 15 points from seven years prior. Hospitals (the people who are supposed to be saving your life) got only a 29% approval. Airlines managed a 12% rating. Actually, across the board, only a few brands really have off-the-chart approval ratings.[90]

If customer confidence in business is increasingly waning, it makes it even more necessary than ever for companies to instill transparency. This is where the apology letter is an important part in maintaining a brand's story.

In Japanese lore, samurais would often commit suicide to apologize for mistakes. I guess there's no greater apology than taking your own life. In today's world, senior executives and brands in general are expected to be front and center on TV or via social media to answer for their brand's mistakes. It's a lot less extreme than falling on your sword. But at the same time, the effects can be about the same from a professional standpoint.

---

88 The Telegraph, September 5, 2012.

89 In recent years, Ryanair has ranked at the very bottom of the customer satisfaction charts with approval ratings somewhere between 34 and 50%. According to Skytrax ratings as of January 1, 2014, the company received a 3.5 out of 10 on nearly 1900 passenger reviews. (airlinequality.com) So the story being written for Ryanair really is "cheap and crappy" in many ways. Perhaps this is a story that they embrace.

90 *The Harris Poll* ® #149, December 2, 2010.

Perhaps author Nicholas Tavuchis said it best in his 1991 book, *Mea Culpa: A Sociology of Apology and Reconciliation.*

"An apology, no matter how sincere or effective, does not and cannot undo what has been done. And yet, in a mysterious way and according to its own logic, this is precisely what it manages to do."

The challenges of writing a proper apology letter are very much the same as many of the techniques that we discussed in earlier chapters.

Step 1: Start With Empathy

One of the worst things a company can do when addressing a crisis is to start from the standpoint of "how much money is this going to cost?" or "how do we reduce the costs of our apology?" If we assume that the world of today is mostly untrusting and that most people think of businesses as faceless, unfeeling centers of unfettered greed, you do need to establish some sense of humanity and humility. Focusing on *your* needs as the baseline to how you speak to your customers is probably a bad start.

Again, go back to the basic theory of empathy and use the "So What?" method to dig down to the real damage that your mistake might have caused. You have to get to the root of the problem and figure out what basic measures of human dignity your mistakes might have set off. In the Ryanair case, a woman who is on perhaps a once-a-year vacation with her family, including three children, might have been unable for some reason to print her tickets. Her issue is not that she's getting charged but rather she can't figure out how in the midst of all the stresses she probably faces as a mom handling a family on vacation, that printing a simple piece of paper should cost more than her tickets. She feels that she is not being treated like a human being. This is perhaps the most raw and worst feeling a person can experience.

An alternative approach might have been that even though the rules are the rules, you could start with a response that provides some dignity to the person and acknowledges what *they* might be feeling.

"We recognize that this guest had a lot to go through. Taking a family on vacation isn't easy. Sometimes we forget to do certain things or just don't have a chance. We feel badly that in this case, our policy on printing boarding cards came across as extremely harsh."

Step 2: Talk About Your Business as Being Human Too

One of the mistakes that businesses often make in telling their story is to forget the fact that they are human beings serving human beings. One of the outgrowths of the "a company's only mission is to make money" management school is that it tends to treat a business as an inanimate object. This is a huge mistake if you look at business storytelling. Empathy works both ways and one of the classical aspects of any dispute is that there are at least two sides that are aggrieved. In the court of public opinion, when a human takes on an inanimate "object", the human will always win. But when a human takes on a business that is also talking about itself in human terms, the outcome is much less settled.

So as compared to Mr. O'Leary's "we're here to reduce costs and make money and therefore the passenger is an idiot" argument, he might have tried to humanize his business.

"One of the basic promises that we try to uphold at Ryanair is to make flying as affordable as possible. To do this, we have to keep costs at a basic minimum. This is a reality because failing to do that means we would eventually go out of business and not be able to provide our service to the community. Millions of people would have to pay more or perhaps forego vacations with their family because they could not affordably fly to their dream destinations. Hiring staff to print everyone's boarding pass would cost us something like $x million per year, a cost that would have to be passed on to passengers. So for us, the issue is how to achieve our mission and help the greatest number of people. Sadly, some people do lose in the process."

On the surface, this requires a lot more words than simply saying "we need to keep costs down". Thankfully, in the modern age of the internet, we have been unshackled by the space limits that printed publications used to impose on us. As such, you can spend a few more words to try to convey a bit more empathy. I like to say, longer answers are harder to read, but at least they show you took the time to care.

Step 3: Propose the Solution

In the end, you have to make a decision on how to solve the problem. While using The Golden Rule ("Do Unto Others As You Would Want Them To Do To You") would be best, ultimately the company has to make a decision based on its priorities.

At least in steps 1 and 2, the apology letter acknowledges the customer's concerns in a very human way. It also achieves the goal of reinforcing "what really matters" to the business on a human level. The idea that a business is important to society in some way at least re-frames how people see the company. They might not like it, but they have to grudgingly accept that your brand maybe isn't some faceless, evil empire.

If your solution lives up to the standards that you've set as a part of society (even if it doesn't make everyone happy), at the very least people know what you represent. This is important because transparency allows you to frame the conversation in your words and not allow others to dictate who you are.

We discussed earlier how the failure of Mitt Romney's campaign team to address efforts to de-humanize him led to his eventual defeat. The same thing happens in business too. Yet sometimes a brand can re-affirm the importance of its product to society while displaying a sense of care for all their consumers through an apology. The recovery of the Tylenol brand after the tainting crisis of 1982 is probably one of the most famous cases of this happening. Addressing people directly has the potential to allow a brand to not only re-win the trust of society, but to make that trust even stronger.

So how does this relate to a brand's story? After all, apologies seem more like the domain of customer service experts.

It's true that most of what I've prescribed is very similar to what countless trainers have taught for decades in terms of how to resolve customer issues. The point is that writing and storytelling and perpetuating a brand's journey need to be viewed from a greater context than ever before.

Storytelling does not exist in a vacuum with customer service in one silo and storytellers in another. Brands are characters in our lives, just as people. Some people pass in and out of our lives and we barely remember them. But when a brand tells its story in a way that it can be accepted as a trusted friend in our lives, we start to relate to them. We remember them for how they helped us and we also remember how they apologized when they made us feel bad too. How they recovered and grew stronger becomes a rallying point for reinforcing what they really represent. It adds credibility when they tell us how they are important to our lives. There's major value in that.

EIGHTEEN

THE FINAL COUNTDOWN
So What Have We Learned?

ALONZO: I'm trying to read. Please shut up.

JAKE: I'll like not being in a hot black and white all summer.

ALONZO: Tell me a story, Hoyt.

JAKE: Like my story?

ALONZO: Not your story, a story. Since you can't shut up so I can read, tell me a story.

JAKE: I don't know any.

ALONZO: You don't?

JAKE: No.

ALONZO: I'll tell you one. This is a newspaper, right? It's 100% bullshit. But it's entertaining. So I read it. It entertains me. You won't let me read it, so you entertain me. Tell me a story now! GO!!

- Training Day (2001)[91]

---

91 Training Day. Dir. Antoine Fuqua. Warner Bros. Pictures, 2001.

Denzel Washington is one of my all-time favorite actors and one of the greatest actors of his generation. In 2002, Washington became the second African-American to ever win an Academy Award for Best Actor, thanks to his performance in "Training Day" in which he played the twisted, sadistic narcotics detective Alonzo Harris.

While Washington's character was some kind of evil, you couldn't help but really like him, perhaps more than the protagonist Jake Hoyt (played by a clearly outclassed Ethan Hawke). I mean, this guy was one motherf***a with some serious street cred. He was so bad, he was just downright the coolest character on the planet.

Writers aren't a whole lot different than actors in a way. In order to get ready for a role, actors go to great lengths to get into character, even when the character is neither like themselves in general nor like any character they have played before. The greatest actors or actresses can play all kinds of roles, romantic, dramatic, comedic and so on. To get ready for a new character, some actors may gain weight, others will lose weight and yet others will tag along with real-life people who actually do the jobs of the characters they intend to play.

The key point behind this is that there is a significant psychological aspect that goes into becoming a great actor or actress. The same goes for those who write stories. Research is important but so is being in the right frame of mind.

Great actors also become known for their ability to evolve. Storytelling is much the same way. The art of telling a business story is no longer about how many ads you can buy or whipping out large numbers of function-related press releases as perhaps it once was. It's no longer about writing to satisfy reporters, but rather finding a way to connect to customers, defining the story in a way that takes on a life of its own in their minds and then forces reporters to take notice after the story has taken root. Storytelling is now about blogs and apology letters, manifestos and "About Us" sections. It's about writing *for* the people instead of *at* the people. In short, storytelling is no longer about marketing; it's about marketing AND basic human psychology. It's about planting desire instead of demanding attention. It's about telling everything instead of just what sells. It's about allowing our customers into the very soul of our brand, just as we allow our close friends to intimately know us.

In the beginning of this book, I talked about getting storytelling into your head. I started with passion. It is impossible to get others to love your story if you don't believe it. Then we talked about empathy and the idea of trying to relate to the internal desires of your customers outside of how they use your product or brand. Finally, we put it together:

Passion + Empathy = Storytelling Success.

We then talked about you can bridge the way you are as a person to the story you are trying to tell on behalf of others:

Inner Voice + Business Voice = Storytelling Success

This assumes that your Inner Voice is your normal natural persona whereas your Business Voice is that role that your company and brand is asking you to play. In a sense it's a process of sync'ing.

In order to become relatable, one theme that we developed over the course of the book was the fallacy of the "98% Rule" and espoused the idea of an "Inverse 98% Rule" in which we understand that we have to consciously win people in order to get them to not only read our story but to believe in it as well.

Now that you were emotionally and psychologically stoked to tell a story we started to talk about some actual tips and tricks to becoming a great storyteller. In a sense, perpetuating a great story has a lot to do with starting the story from the beginning. This is where the concept of a journey comes in. I talked about the various steps that need to be included in your journey, the idea, the process, the end result and, in certain cases, that awesome event where the journey continues to write itself over and over. I talked about the incredible impact of founders' stories as a basis for the idea to make the journey that much more powerful. And we saw how personalizing the story, talking from the perspective of a real person as opposed to simply putting a faceless corporate voice to your storytelling, can also add to your relatability factor.

Then we got to the lift-off stage. This is where you really write the story. I talked about how to find your "real story" by employing the "So What?" technique, a method of pushing you to find why your brand or company is really so important in the grand scheme of the universe. I talked about tone and the importance of creating a voice that was relatable for followers of your brand. I talked about how to use the first person to create a greater connection and how to envision people "nodding their heads" when you write.

Once you have invited them into your world, you can effectively employ the "ST Rule", the idea that superlatives are an integral part of your story but also one that needs to be applied with a measure of caution. Credibility is key and if you overdo it, you risk losing the plot in your story. In any event, the "ST Rule" ensures that your story embodies some grander mission that people can join. If you add together bringing people on The Journey, you can then start to talk about the true enormity of what you are trying to bring the world. This basically wraps up the belief element of your story. Once you have gained that credibility, you've mostly won the battle. At the same time, I talked about the idea of the cynical customer and how to reframe your story in such a way to strengthen the message without crossing the line to overhype. This is where the $40 Steak and Fries Rule comes into play.

In the last part of the book, I talked about some approaches that are a little bit beyond the classic press release. In fact, our manifestos, our blogs, our apology letters and our "About Us" sections on our website are not merely random tools that are the exclusive domain of our human resources, customer service or PR departments. In an organization, storytelling needs to be considered something much more holistic, crossing beyond the traditional silos. Part of bringing people on a journey comes in using these different types of communications toward creating a richer story.

The common thread of this entire book is the idea that organizations need to re-think the way they do business, emphasizing a deeper level of trust, commitment and even love with the people they serve as well as the people who work for them. Business is no longer a three-dimensional exercise; it's actually now four-dimensional with storytelling as an integral part of everything that happens.

By the same token, for anyone thinking of starting a career in the marketing field, it's perhaps time to start forgetting the established tenets envisaged by the so-called "gurus" of years ago. The world today is a very different place. The age of using doubt, fear and manipulation are over. It is still possible to be a good marketer without being a great storyteller. But to become a great marketer, developing an ability to envisage and write a great story is essential. Writing isn't the only way of course. Photographers, designers and filmmakers (or perhaps better yet, YouTubers) have a certain sub-set of skills that can be equally powerful to a great writer. In truth, we need storytellers across all kinds of mediums. But for those who are a bit more inclined to the written word and for those looking for the bigger picture, I hope this book has helped you get just one step closer to being a citizen of the Four-Dimensional World.

ACKNOWLEDGMENTS

In many ways, this book is a kind of culmination of much of my career to this point. Certainly, I could not have reached this point without the advice and support of a great number of very special people, each of whom has, in their own way, contributed to the body of this book.

I owe an eternal debt of gratitude to my wonderful parents, Joshua and Eileen Mendelsohn, who sacrificed so much to give me all the tools and opportunities in life to make what I could out of it and showed great patience with me even when I made choices that were quite difficult for them to accept. Among many other valuable lessons, my parents taught me that the care and pride you put into your endeavors is a reflection of who you are as a person. This is a lesson that I think only the luckiest children ever receive.

I also owe so much to the world's greatest sister, Dr. Laurie Mendelsohn-Levin, who has always been my biggest supporter and her husband, Dr. Adam Levin, who is a great friend as well as an incredible brother-in-law.

To Irwan Mussry and Victor and Michelle Sassoon, who invited me into their home many years ago and took a chance on me when few others would. They taught me what it was like to win in my career and in life without ever sacrificing my personal identity. Many of the stories in this book could never have come about were it not for their continuous faith in me. A special thanks goes out as well to Mel Elias who, prior to running the empire that is Coffee Bean & Tea Leaf, was kind enough to welcome a stranger to his family and has been a friend ever since.

A further thanks to Shannon Hartono who has been like a partner in my own development for so many years and to Emlyn Siswanto, Pieter Sugiyanto, Surianto Syarif, Alvin Pangestu and Hidayat Hamzah, who have taught me far more than I could ever have possibly taught them. Most of the thinking behind this book was incubated based on our shared experiences over many years in Time International. I've been very lucky to work with so many wonderful team members at the company and each of them has taught me something new each and every day.

Over the years, I've been honored to be associated with some wonderful leaders who have helped to shape my view of the world. I owe a lot to Steve Alley of the U.S. Foreign Commercial Service, a great friend and supporter as I started out my career in Malaysia. Bill Shurniak, a dear family friend for many years, gave me a chance to get my feet wet in retail in A.S. Watson & Company. His incredible generosity allowed me the chance to overcome a difficult introduction to the professional world when I was far from home for the very first time.

There are a great many friends who started out as business acquaintances but over time became so much more. Brian Fernandez, Sivapalan Vivekarajah and Chris Chan were all people who showed incredible faith in me when I was still a struggling entrepreneur and taught me how to see the big picture. Rasheed Shroff of Fossil Asia Pacific has been a great friend and business partner for so many years, as well as an inspiration in courage, even if he is always too humble to admit it. Jeff Anderson of Rip Curl Asia Pacific has been an equally terrific partner and someone who has given me so many ideas on the importance of organizational culture and the power of always trying something new. DJ and entrepreneur Anton Wirjono has been a valued friend and a person who inspires me to think of something new each and every time I see him. Career coach Rene Suhardono has opened my eyes to many incredible views of the world and life even in the short time that I've known him.

Ram Kumar has always given me an inspiring perspective on the importance of even the most basic things in life. I owe a great deal to Munshir Abdullah, who helped me formulate business strategies for so long through handwritten messages on the back of old cigarette cartons. Eric Cohen is not only a lifelong friend but also played a major role in helping me make a major transition in my life more than a decade ago.

A huge thanks goes out to Ronnie Singh of 2K Games who was so incredibly gracious and supportive to a person he met only through cyberspace. You were a role model for me before I wrote this book and learning more about your story provided me with even more inspiration.

To Edward Suhadi who demonstrated that it's never too late to find the right path. His writing inspires me and a lot of others. His story is one that I've always felt showed incredible conviction and courage.

I also want to give a special thank you to those who helped me to finally get this book to print. Thank you to my editor Roy Simson, my designer Anida Dyah and to Ollie and Windy Ariestanty, who provided some terrific input on how to navigate the final steps of this process.

And of course, last but not least to my eternally beautiful wife Joe and our gregarious little son Liam, who makes me smile and amazes me each and every time we are together. Joe and I have shared so many incredible memories together and she was so patient in allowing me the time and freedom to write this book. Her uncompromising support for my career and my life has made me better in more ways than I could ever say. For many years, I questioned whether the perfect soul mate even existed. She has proved to be that and so much more for me.

And of course I owe a great debt to you, the reader, for your support. I very much look forward to hearing your comments. Please send any comments, questions or stories via Twitter to @waliwali1 or by email to waliwali01@yahoo.com.

INDEX

www.ingramcontent.com/pod-product-compliance
Lightning Source LLC
Chambersburg PA
CBHW060026210326
41520CB00009B/1012